THE
REAL
SELF

**A Developmental, Self,
and Object Relations Approach**

By James F. Masterson, M.D.

THE
REAL
SELF

A Developmental, Self,
and Object Relations Approach

Structure
    Function
        Development
            Psychopathology
                Treatment
                    Creativity

By **James F. Masterson, M.D.**

 Brunner/Mazel *Publishers* • New York

THIRD PRINTING

Library of Congress Cataloging in Publication Data

Masterson, James F.
  The real self.

  Bibliography: p.
  Includes index.
  1. Personality, Disorders of. 2. Self.
I. Title. [DNLM: 1. Ego. 2. Personality Development.
3. Psychoanalytic Theory. 4. Psychotherapy.
WM 460.5.E3 M423r]
RC554.M275 1985   616.89   85-12824
ISBN 0-87630-400-5

Copyright © 1985 by James F. Masterson

Published by
BRUNNER/MAZEL, INC.
19 Union Square West
New York, New York 10003

MANUFACTURED IN THE UNITED STATES OF AMERICA

Acknowledgments

I would like to thank Mrs. J. Kelly for typing the manuscript, and my wife for filling in when necessary. In addition, I would like to thank my colleague, E. T. Carlson, M.D., psychiatrist and historian, for his stimulation and interest in the study of Thomas Wolfe and Jean Paul Sartre. Finally, I am grateful to Ralph Klein, M.D., and Candace Orcuff, Ph.D., for their helpful suggestions on the manuscript.

James F. Masterson

Contents

PART 3. CREATIVITY AND THE REAL SELF

Part 1

THEORY AND CLINICAL WORK

CHAPTER I

Acknowledgment of the Emerging Real Self

The real self emerges in early intrapsychic development, grows throughout latency and adolescence, and then in adulthood must be articulated in reality. This search to consciously identify and express the real self may involve many changes in external behavior over a long period of time. If the expression is appropriate, it reinforces and strengthens the inner real self in circular feedback fashion. However, unarticulated aspects of the real self may lie dormant for many years, only to surface in surprising ways in later life.

Malcolm Cowley (1984), referring to writing his memoirs at age 85, said,

When I was a college student and I heard other students asking "Who am I," I listened to them with sympathy but also with a measure of disdain. When I was their age I knew damn well who I was. Now, however, I am not so certain. Since I am 85 the question comes back to me, if in a slightly different form—'Who was I'—and the answer is not always what I had expected. If this memoir in which I am engaged has accomplished its task I shall have discovered or unveiled a shape in time. I shall have revealed to myself the person who is possibly the real me. (p.1)

In addition, he may still uncover some new unarticulated aspects of his real self.

The ideas presented in this volume are not "revealed knowledge" and did not spring full grown like Athena from the head of Zeus. They emerged from a long, slow, often laborious and tedious professional struggle which required the grappling with and resolution of both personal conflicts and professional challenges. The personal struggle involved in developing and refining these theoretical and clinical ideas helped me, like Malcolm Cowley, to more precisely refine and define, as well as fulfill, my real self.

In retrospect, it seems that I have been hovering over or circling around the emotional problems of the self for some 30 years, gradually working through and trying to master the outer layers of the problem in order to probe the core—a concept of the real self and its disorders. For example, I began my work at the most superficial layer—a descriptive approach to the diagnostic problems of personality disorders in adolescence (Masterson, 1967). This led to the next layer—a psychoanalytic approach that shifted the focus of study of the personality disorders from adolescence to the first three years of life (Masterson, 1972). The vehicle for this penetration to a deeper layer was the linking of an understanding of normal separation-individuation with object relations theory (Mahler, 1975; Mahler & McDevitt, 1982; Masterson, 1967, 1972, 1976, 1980, 1981, 1983).

However, although acknowledgment was given to the self tangentially in this theory of separation-individuation, the perspective emphasized object relations, not the self. The self seemed to tag along just for the sake of completion. The confusion in psychoanalytic theories of the self only seemed to compound the problem. The conceptual gap was unsatisfactorily filled by concepts of the ego and ego identity. Nevertheless, dramatic improvements in understanding of the patient's problems and in psychotherapy emerged from all these developments. Yet the core remained elusive, the nettle was not being grasped.

Despite this, the self continued to make its clinical presence felt and to press for further attention. In our follow-up study of treated borderline adolescents (Masterson, 1980), the importance of self-image, self-activation and self-assertion stood out like a neon sign. At the same time, for reasons I have described elsewhere, Kohut's notion of the self (1971, 1977), particularly its therapeutic implications for the borderline patient, seemed to me to leave a great deal to be desired.

I found myself, without intention or plan, focusing more and more in my work with patients on the patient's self to the point of spontaneously developing one symbol [s] when the patient was activating his or her real self in the session and another [o] for the relationship with objects. I began thinking and talking more and more in terms of a real and defensive self as it became clearer and clearer in the clinical material. Only after I had been using this concept of the self in psychotherapy for several years did I finally decide that I had to think it through further, organize it and describe it if only to clarify it for myself and to get it out of my system. This clarification also helped to further define the use and function of the therapeutic technique of communicative matching which I had described before but not fully developed.

This 30-year quest has clarified and reinforced my own professional real self which has now in this book led to a theory that hopefully can help others to clarify and define their selves. This theory shifts the focus—the microscope of observation and study—in development and disorder from the object—object relations—to the self; instead of thinking primarily in terms of objects and ego, we can think of the self with its objects and its ego. After all, in our daily toil with our patients, our work revolves around a person with a self, not a collection of objects and an ego.

This book adds to and in some respects is a culmination of my prior work in developmental object relations theory. Therefore, it cannot be considered apart from all that work. Substantial distortions could occur if the reader were to read only this book or attempt to understand it apart from that larger body of work.

Chapter II briefly summarizes psychoanalytic theories of the self, to help the reader place the developmental object relations theory of the self presented in Chapter III in a broader context. Chapters IV and V present the disorders of the self and their treatment—communicative matching. This material, the backbone of the book, derives from close intense observation, testing and retesting of clinical hypotheses with a large number of patients over many years and thus carries its own weight of clinical validity.

This clinically derived perspective on the real self, rooted in early developmental concepts, came to animate my entire outlook and to impel my curiosity, also, towards how the attitudes of various cultures toward child raising affected the development of a real self. This was stimulated by reading Bettleheim's (1969) book *Children of the Dream* about an Israeli kibbutz. It appeared to me that kibbutz child-rearing attitudes contrasted with child-raising attitudes in the United States and therefore were a good example of how different attitudes toward child rearing had different effects on the development of the real self.

I then had the opportunity to travel in Japan where I noted that Japanese attitudes to child rearing differed from those in both Israel and the United States and had a still different effect on the development of the real self. These ideas, speculative and hypothetical as compared to the clinical ideas in prior chapters, are presented in Chapter VI.

This interest in how the "character" of cultures affected the development of the real self led naturally to an interest in how contemporary cultural values affected adult functioning of the real self. These concepts are presented in Chapter VII.

Any psychotherapist who works with patients with preoedipal fixations or disorders of the self, if his treatment is successful, is forced to confront the issue of creativity as his patient's self emerges and becomes creative. Beyond that, an interest in the theory of the function of the real self leads inevitably to an interest in creativity—the ultimate of self expression. I became interested in the creative experiences of the self—in the fairytales used to guide the child's emerging self and, more importantly, in how artists use their creativity in the search to articulate a real self. As an adolescent I was fascinated by Thomas Wolfe's novels (1929, 1934, 1935, 1936, 1937) without knowing why. Years later, as a psychiatrist, when I came to understand the role of the abandonment depression in the developmental arrest of the self, curiosity about his work returned because he seemed to be the perfect novelist of separation-individuation and the borderline personality disorder. His writings contained haunting, poetic, elegiac evocations of the affect of abandonment depression. His work was so autobiographical that it was a short step to study his life where I found that he used his creativity, his writing, in a desperate, perhaps lifesaving, effort to find a real self, as described in Chapters IX and X.

I came to Sartre (1946, 1964) and Munch (Eggum, 1983; Stang, 1977) from a different angle, having had only a tangential prior interest in their work. At about the same time as I was becoming aware of the emotional significance of Thomas Wolfe's novels as an expression of his abandonment depression, I also had an idea that Sartre's philosophy was perhaps an intellectual rationalization of an abandonment depression, i.e., it's not that I feel alone, helpless and depressed but that's the way life is. Similarly, I felt many of Munch's paintings were vivid portraits of abandonment depression. These ideas on Sartre and Munch are presented in summary in Chapter VIII as contrasting examples of creativity used in an effort to establish a real self.

The reader should keep in mind that Chapters VI, IX, and X are not presented as cross-cultural, cultural or psychobiographical studies in their own right. Rather the material is used to extend and elaborate the clinical concept of the real self.

Chapter XI presents a summary and discussion. The thesis of the book, derived from child observation studies of normal development and from clinical psychotherapeutic work with borderline and narcissistic personality disorders, is that for the self to fully emerge from the symbiotic union and assume its full capacities, identification, acknowledgment and support are required—from the mother and father in early development and from the therapist in psychotherapy.

There may be some children whose capacity for individuation is so great that they do not need external acknowledgment, and others whose capacity is so weak that no amount of external acknowledgment will suffice; but most children will be somewhere in between. As for borderline and narcissistic personality disorder patients, their developmental arrest is generally related, along with other possible factors, to environmental failure to acknowledge and support the patient's real self.

The importance of this issue in psychotherapy of borderline and narcissistic personality disorders has been obscured until recently because object relations theory has heretofore placed too great an emphasis on object relations and too little on a concept of the self. This effort to redress that imbalance can be seen as an addition to, rather than an attempt to replace, the prior emphasis.

The added perspective on the self provides additional focus for both observation and intervention; it rounds out and completes our understanding of the psychopathology. Beyond that, it focuses the clinical work closer to the patient's experience of distress and provides a more immediate vocabulary for communication —i.e., the phrase self-activation or self-expression is far more immediate, relevant and closer to the patient's emotional experience than the more abstract term—individuate.

The therapist's technique for acknowledgment of the real self is called *communicative matching*. It is an art, a matter of delicacy of fit and timing like a good interpretation. If used by itself, it will be regressive and self-destructive, but when combined with the other therapeutic techniques of confrontation, interpretation, etc., that contain the transference acting-out and promote the working through of depression, it provides the necessary added dimension to create the conditions for an optimum repair of the impaired real self. Not that a substantial improvement cannot take place without it, but that improvement will not reach its optimum.

I cannot caution enough about the principal distortions of this view of communicative matching. The first consists of those therapists whose view of therapeutic neutrality is so fixed and rigid that it permits no such interventions. Their patients may improve if the rest of the approach is appropriate, but they will not reach the optimum.

I am far more concerned about the other, far more common distortion that exaggerates this view of communicative matching to be a license for cheerleading the patient's self-activation. This happens, it seems to me, most often with therapists who project their own countertransference helplessness on the patient and then try to guide or direct the patient out of it. Let me re-emphasize that this leads to disaster as it perpetuates the patient's regressive rewarding object-relations unit defenses.

One cannot direct, order, flatter, dominate, threaten, coerce, seduce or otherwise force a patient to activate his real self or individuate. One can only create the conditions that make it possible. The patient must take it from there. Self-activation means exactly what it says.

The key here is *balance*. The communicative matching is effective only when properly integrated in balance with the rest of the work and when done from a position of therapeutic neutrality and objectivity. The therapist is a servant of the process that goes on in the patient's psyche. He or she must be guided by that process. The chapters that follow illustrate the use of communicative matching to facilitate the emergence and consolidation of the real self. Chapter II sets the stage by a brief review of psychoanalytic theories of the self.

CHAPTER II

Psychoanalytic Theories
of the Self: A Brief Summary

Theories of the self have led to more confusion than understanding in the development of psychoanalytic thinking. Freud's
ambiguous use of the term ICH to refer to the self both as a whole
person—subjective experiential—and to the ego (as translated by
Strachey, 1966)—theoretical, more objective and mechanical—led
to considerable confusion about the relationship between the self
and the ego which persists to this day.

The matter was further confused (according to Bettelheim, 1982)
by the abstract mistranslations of Freud's vital words.

BETTELHEIM ON FREUD

Bettelheim (1982) noted that in his work and in his writings,
Freud often spoke of the soul—of its nature and structure, its
development, its attributes, how it reveals itself in all we do and
dream. Unfortunately, nobody who reads him in English could
guess this, because nearly all his many references to the soul, and

to matters pertaining to the soul, have been excised in translation. In the 1933 *New Introductory Lectures on Psychoanalysis*, in the chapter titled "The Dissection of the Psychical Personality," Freud (1964), speaking of the *I,* the *it*, and the *above-I*, describes them as "the three provinces of the apparatus of the soul." In *The Question of Lay Analysis* (1959), the phrase is translated as "the three provinces of the mental apparatus (p. 71)." And in conceptualizing the workings of the psyche, distinguishing the conscious from the unconscious, and distinguishing the functions of the *I*, and the *above-I*, Freud uses the term "soul" to describe what he regards as the overarching concept that takes in all the others. In various places (1959), he spoke about "the structure of the soul" and "the organization of the soul." In the translation, these terms are almost always rendered as "mental apparatus" or "mental organization." Almost invariably, the *Standard Edition*, like the earlier English translations, either omits Freud's references to the soul or translates them as if he spoke only of man's mind. Freud never faltered in his conviction that it was important to think in terms of the soul when trying to comprehend his system.

Where Freud selected a word that, used in daily parlance, makes us feel vibrantly alive, the translations present us with a term from a dead language that reeks of erudition precisely when it should emanate vitality. To refer to the unknown, unconscious contents of the mind, he chose the personal pronoun "it" (*es*) and used it as a noun (*das Es*). This was translated as "id." To mistranslate ICH as "ego" is to transform it into jargon that no longer conveys the personal commitment we make when we say "I" or "me," not to mention our subconscious memories of the deep emotional experience we had when, in infancy, we discovered ourselves as we learned to say "I."

In creating the concept of the ICH, Freud tied it to reality by using a term that made it practically impossible to leave reality behind. Reading or speaking about the "I" forces one to look at oneself introspectively. By contrast, an "ego" that uses clear-cut mechanisms, such as displacement and projection, to achieve its purpose in its struggle against the "id" is something that can be studied from the outside by observing others. When I say "I," I mean my entire self, my total personality. Freud made an important distinction here. What he called the "I" refers primarily to the conscious, rational aspects of oneself. It gives us the intuitive feeling that Freud is right to name the "I" what we feel to be our true self, even though we know that we do not always act in line with that self.

OTHER ANALYTIC VIEWS OF THE SELF AND THE EGO

An additional factor contributing to the confusion was that Freud and the pioneer analysts worked mostly with neurosis and, therefore, with oedipal levels of conflict. This is a developmental level at which the self had already become autonomous and assumed its functions and capacities; as a result, it did not cause enough of the kind of clinical problems that might have drawn attention. It was not crucial for these early analysts to focus on a concept of the self; they could take it for granted as it "worked." This caused some loss in the sense that not enough attention was paid to the subjective experiential and creative aspects of the self. Not that they weren't noted, but they were seen more as a by-product of successful treatment of the neurosis. In other words, these analysts could go about their work comfortably, unhampered by not having a well developed concept of the self. It was not a central issue of pathology in their patients.

However, when analysts turned their attention to patients with psychoses and character disorders, the sense of comfort disappeared. These patients' development was arrested not at the oedipal but at the preoedipal level and, therefore, their deep difficulties were predominantly with the functioning of the self. The lack of a fully developed concept of the self, which had not previously been an obstacle, now became one.

Freud and Jung

This professional, theoretical issue—how patients with a preoedipal developmental arrest differed from those with an oedipal conflict—was an important factor, in addition to interpersonal conflict, in the conflict that arose between Jung and Freud in 1912 which produced a dramatic schism in the psychoanalytic movement of the time. This schism was further extended and elaborated by others and continues to this very day.

Jung, who had probably had a psychotic attack himself during his own development, was primarily interested in psychotics whose principal conflicts he felt were preoedipal; therefore, he found the classical oedipal theory of the time not as helpful. This led him to his interest in a concept of the self (1973b). He saw psychosis as primarily a conflict involving the self at the preoedipal level, while Freud insisted that it was a regression from an oedipal-level conflict (McGuire, 1974; Jung, 1973b). While Jung was probably closer to the truth than Freud at that time, a more modern view of schizophrenia would stress its organic nature. However, as so often happens with theoreticians, Jung later went on to make the same mistake as Freud by trying to extend his basically preoedipal notion of the self forward developmentally to explain oedipal conflict in neurosis.

It is also interesting to speculate on the personal motivations for this conflict between these two giants. Freud had had an affectionate relationship with his father but had felt that his father was not a success in the world and that his own success represented a triumph over his father. He became concerned that others, i.e., his peers, might do the same to him and, therefore, he was a stickler for others adhering to his theoretical views. Jung, on the other hand, with a successful father with whom he was not close, feared that the father would attempt to indoctrinate him with the father's views. Inevitably, these two dynamic themes clashed in Jung and Freud's relationship and made their own contribution to the split (McGuire, 1974).

From this basic conflict there emerged two mainstreams of thought with regard to the concept of the self, each of which emphasized one of the two senses in which Freud used the term—either the whole person or as a special part of the mind with its own unique capacities and functions. Those who emphasized ICH as ego tended to be working mostly with neurotics and oedipal conflicts and placed heavy emphasis on the structural theory (ego, id, superego). They tended to emphasize the objective and the theoretical and sometimes could seem quite mechanistic, placing less emphasis on the subjective, experiential and creative aspects of the self.

Those who emphasized the other meaning of the term ICH—the self as the whole person—tended to be working with psychoses and character disorders, and preoedipal levels of conflict and difficulties with the self. They placed less emphasis on the objective and theoretical aspects and more on the subjective, personal and experiential. The emphasis of this group on the self, almost to the detriment of the unconscious and the more theoretical objective aspects of the functioning of the mind, similarly caused a loss in terms of both depth and objectivity.

This latter group who emphasized the self as a whole person further fractionated into a number of subgroups based on varying definitions of the self, its nature and its functions as follows:

Jung (1953, 1973a, 1973b). Jung saw the self as a primordial image or archetype expressing the individual's need for unity, wholeness and its highest aspirations. His treatment objective was self-realization and self-fulfillment. The unconscious was downgraded in importance by being divided into a collective and a personal unconscious. His treatment was also of short duration, less frequency and less depth.

Rank (1929). Rank focused on the psychological aspects of the emergence of the physical self at birth and emphasized separation anxiety as springing from birth trauma. His treatment emphasized the need to work through the deeply repressed anxiety about the birth trauma; it was generally of short duration, less frequency and, of course, less depth.

Adler (1940). Adler saw the life-style (repetitive patterns derived from early childhood) as a defensive overcompensation for inferiority feelings about the self, therefore blocking the emergence of the real, creative self. His treatment, too, was short, less frequent and of less depth.

Horney (1946, 1950). She postulated an idealized self which produced a pseudo unity or wholeness that blocked the emergence of what she called the real self.

Sullivan (in Mullahy, 1970). He felt that the essence of the self was determined by its functions: (1) the fulfillment of needs; (2) the maintenance of security.

It was perhaps inevitable that the analysts working primarily with a concept of the self as a whole person would become fascinated by creativity because, as the patient's difficulties with the self were repaired, the creativity would be freed and emerge. Some, for example, such as Jung and Adler, made this a central objective of treatment. It is interesting to note that each of these analysts had one or more pieces of the psychological puzzle correctly.

A reconciliation of both senses of the use of the word ICH or self—whole person and ego—has more recently been undertaken by theoreticians in ego psychology and object relations theory. Hartmann (1958, 1964) distinguished between the self as a whole person, the ego as a system (part of the tripartite structure of id, ego, superego), and the self representation as the intrapsychic representation of the self. He also defined narcissism as the libidinal investment of the self representation. Then Jacobson (1964), in order to work with psychotics, carried the concept further by defining the self representation as the unconscious, preconscious and conscious intrapsychic representations of the bodily and mental self in the system ego. Kernberg (1982) used the term character to refer to the self as a whole person and preferred to use the term self to refer to the sum total of intrapsychic self representations in intimate contact with the sum total of object representations in the ego. In contrast to Hartmann, he felt that the self and object representations are both libidinally and aggressively invested.

Kohut

Kohut (1971, 1977), from his work with narcissistic personality disorders, viewed the self as consisting of fused self objects which were invested with narcissistic libido that had its own line of development separate from the development of object representations and object libido. In other words, there was no separation of self from object, but rather maturation of self-objects from primitive to mature forms. The structure of the self was defined as having its own functions, its own development, and its own pathology. I have commented extensively on Kohut's point of view in another publication (1981) and will only indicate some of my disagreements here.

Kohut's clinical observations of the psychopathology of the self in the Narcissistic Personality Disorder and his ideas on its treatment have been widely accepted, but this theory of a psychology of the self has met with many objections. His theory competes with object relations theory and seems to run contrary to the findings of child observation research that the self separates from the object. Kohut's view of an independent line of development of narcissism as expressed in his concept of the bipolar self—i.e., fused self object—which does not separate but matures from infantile to mature forms, leads to conceptual confusions between the self and the object as part of the self, between the various stages or phases of the early development of the self and object representations, and finally between the differences in degree of psychological input into the developing self of the mother's mirroring function and the father's idealizing function. These theoretical confusions then lead to clinical confusions about the nature of the transference and what level of emotional conflict is being worked through in the treatment. The most important clinical implication of these confusions is that Kohut views what I call the Borderline Personality Disorder as a Narcissistic Personality Disorder, which leads to inappropriate treatment.

A NEW DEFINITION OF THE SELF

This brief historical review brings us to the current situation and raises the question as to why it is necessary to bother with more theoretical baggage? Why more efforts to define a concept of the self? Borderline and narcissistic patients' problems crucially involve the self. Therapists working with these patients are in the very forefront of observation of these difficulties. Mahler, from the perspective of the development of the self, said, "The development of the sense of self is an eminently personal internal experience that is difficult, if not impossible, to trace the beginnings of by observational studies or reconstructions in psychoanalysis. It reveals itself by its failure much more readily than by its normal variations" (Mahler & McDevitt, 1982, p. 847).

The therapist working with these patients is in a unique position to observe these difficulties with the self. Beyond that, as these difficulties are repaired in treatment, this unique vantage point of observations is enhanced as the therapist observes the patient acquire the capacities of his or her real self (including creativity). This is probably the reason that most therapists who work in this area eventually become interested in creativity: the ultimate of real self expression.

My own theoretical perspective on borderline and narcissistic disorders derived from a developmental object relations theory which had placed major emphasis on the link between the gradual unfolding of the separation and individuation process and the growth and maturation of the self and object representations. In the borderline patient particularly, the focus was on therapeutic confrontation of the defense mechanisms against the abandonment depression. This led to overcoming the defenses and the working through of the abandonment depression, which attenuated or overcame the developmental arrest so that the separation individuation process could resume its developmental path. The point of view as reflected in the terms used was heavily weighted towards object relations theory, with a notion of the self implied in the terms separation and individuation. What is it that separates and individuates but the self? However, the emphasis was more on the ICH in the sense of ego rather than on the self.

As the patient worked through his abandonment depression, a consequent event shifted my attention more to notions of the self. The patient would develop a new interest or activity (self-activation or individuation). This activity would again stimulate the abandonment depression even though it appeared that most of it had been worked through. Beyond that, interpretation now was of no help. It appeared to me that this new effort at self expression or activation required something else.

I began a type of intervention that I came to call *communicative matching*—a term derived from Mahler's term *refueling* (1975, 1982)—her description of how the mother provided refueling or support for the child's individuative efforts through responding with nonverbal cues of support to the child's assertive explorations. I used the term in the sense of an effort to discuss with the patient from my own experience a new fantasy and feeling, interest or activity in which he or she was now engaged.

This communicative matching helped to further attenuate the patient's abandonment depression so that the patient's self-expression was reinforced and flowered. At the same time, therapeutic objectivity was maintained and regressive rewarding unit defenses were not activated. In retrospect, it seemed that the acknowledgment and effort to share the self-expression had enabled the patient's self to better integrate and activate new interests and capacities. A refueling of the patient's emerging real self had occurred and new capacities had emerged.

AN ADDITIONAL DIMENSION: A FOCUS ON THE REAL SELF

This led me to focus my attention more and more not only on the abandonment depression and its defenses but also on the difficulties in functioning of the self such as self-image, self-acknowledgment, soothing, self-entitlement, self-assertion, etc. As I did so, it seemed to me that these difficulties in functioning of the self were as important a consequence of the abandonment depression as the ego fixation with its ego defects and primitive mechanisms of defense. There was as much an arrest of development of the self as there was of the ego.

The emerging real self precipitated the depression; the need to defend against that depression prevented the real self from growing and assuming its normal capacities. In psychotherapy, as the abandonment depression was worked through, the real self emerged and slowly acquired its capacities along with the maturation of ego functions, defenses and object relations.

For example, follow-up studies of treatment of borderline adolescents (Masterson, 1980) demonstrated that in those who improved there was progressive incremental improvement in the functioning of the self, which acquired new capacities.

These observations could easily tempt one to take the route of earlier workers who defined the self as the whole person and focused on that to the exclusion of the intrapsychic dimension, object relations, ego defenses, the unconscious, etc.

However, this additional dimension of a focus on the self (defined as an intrapsychic entity), when kept in concert with the other perspectives of developmental object relations theory, can lead to a broader, more inclusive and comprehensive concept of the borderline and narcissistic disorders as disorders of the self.

This view reconciles both definitions of ICH—the self and the ego—bringing together the personal, subjective experiential with the objective, mechanistic theoretical.

Beyond that, in clinical work the use of the concept of the self and its difficulties in functioning seems to me to be a more precise, economic, efficient and useful tool to bring to the patient's attention that it is his own efforts at self expression and activation that bring on the depression that activates the defense. It is remarkable to note the extraordinary degree to which we all unconsciously assume that self-expression is naturally positive, gratifying and nonconflictual—in other words, a denial of crucial conflicts that we have about self-expression.

In addition, a concept of a normal autonomous self with its own development and its own capacities helps to cast in bold relief the psychopathology of the self produced by borderline and narcissistic disorder patients, i.e., the deformed formations of the self representations used to defend against the separation anxiety and abandonment depression experienced by the activation of the real self. The next chapter describes the structure, functioning, and development of the real self.

CHAPTER III

The Real Self: Structure and Development

A few definitions will facilitate discussion of the structure of the real self.

Self-image

The image an individual has of himself at a particular time and in a specific situation. It consists of his body image and the mental representation of his state at the time. This image may be conscious or unconscious, realistic or distorted (Moore & Fine, 1968).

Self Representation

A more enduring schema than self-image, constructed by the ego out of the multitude of realistic and distorted self images which an individual has had at different times. It represents the

20

person as he consciously and unconsciously perceives himself and may be dormant or active (Moore & Fine, 1968).

Supraordinate Self-organization

Because subjective experiences may be organized by multiple self representations, the "I" of one state of mind may not necessarily be the same as the "I" of another state of mind. This term is used for the organization and patterning of the various subordinate self-images and representations (Horowitz & Zilber, 1983). It connects them and provides a continuity between them and a sense of unity and wholeness.

The Total Self

The total person of an individual in reality, including his body and psychic organization; one's own person as contrasted with other persons and objects outside oneself. A commonsense concept.

THE REAL SELF

In keeping with ego psychology and object relations theory, the term "real self" is used here not as the total self but in the intrapsychic sense of the sum of self and object representations with their related affects. How can an object representation be defined as part of the self without accepting Kohut's idea of a fused self-object? If it is part of the self, how can it also be separate? When the self and object separate, they mature in parallel, influencing each other's growth. Thus the object representation that develops is uniquely shaped by the self representation just as the self representation is uniquely shaped by the object representation. Both have characteristics unique to that one person. In addition, the self representation also becomes autonomous.

The term "real" is synonymous with healthy or normal. It is used to emphasize that the representations of the real self have an important conscious reality component even though unconscious fantasy elements occur. It also indicates that the real self has an important reality function.

Although I have a number of reservations about Winnicott's (1965) theory of the true and false self, he comes close to describing my notion of the real self in his concept of the true self: "The true self is the theoretical position from which comes the spontaneous gesture and personal idea. The spontaneous gesture is the true self in action. Only the true self can be creative and feel real" (p. 148). I would emphasize that the true or real self has a function in reality as well as feeling real. From the point of view of Erikson (1968), I am referring to the personal self-identity aspect of his concept of identity rather than the ego identity. I view that self-identity from an intrapsychic perspective rather than from Erikson's interpersonal one.

The term real self also helps, as we will see later, to differentiate it from the false selves of the borderline and narcissistic patients that are based primarily on defensive fantasy, not on reality, and are directed toward defense, not toward self-expression in reality. When using the term real self, I will be referring to both the collective subordinate self representations and their supraordinate organization.

The real self exists as a parallel partner of the ego and has its own development, its own capacities, and its own psychopathology. The self and the ego develop and function together in tandem, like two horses in the same harness. If the ego is arrested in development, so is the self. One does not see an arrested ego without an arrested self. One aspect of the self could be viewed as the representational arm of the ego, although it is obviously more than that. Similarly, one aspect of the ego, since it deals with volition and will and with the activation and gratification of individuative wishes, could be viewed as the executive arm of the self. However, it is also obviously more than that as its primary function is maintaining intrapsychic equilibrium.

Erikson (1968) referred to the dual and inseparable nature of the self-ego as follows:

Identity formation can be said to have a self aspect and an ego aspect. What could be called the self identity emerges from experiences from which temporarily confused (subordinate) selves are successfully reintegrated in an ensemble of roles which also secure social recognition. One can speak of ego identity when one discusses the ego's synthesizing power in the light of its central psychosocial function and a self identity when the integration of the individual's self-role images are under discussion. (p. 211)

He elaborated further on the self: "What the I reflects on when it sees or experiences the body, the personality and the roles to which it is attached for life, not knowing where it was before or will be after, are the various selves which make up our composite self." He recommended that psychoanalysts discontinue the use of the word ego when what is meant is the self as an object of the I:

For example, one should speak of an ideal self rather than an ego ideal as the image of what we would like ourselves to be like and the self identity rather than ego identity insofar as the I perceives itself as continuous in time and uniform in sub-stance. When we have separated the self and the I from ego we can reserve for the ego the domain of an inner agency safeguarding our coherent existence by screening and syn-thesizing in any series of moments all the impressions and emotions, memories and impulses which try to enter our thought and demand our action and which would tear us apart if unsorted and unmanaged by a slowly growing and reliable watchful screening system. The self is mostly preconscious but it can be made conscious. In other words, when the self wills it whereas the ego is mostly unconscious and manages to do for us as the heart and brain do what we could never figure out or plan consciously. To ignore the conscious I, the self, in its relations to its existence means to delete the core of human self awareness, the capacity which after all makes self analysis possible.

He elaborated further:

To differentiate between personal identity (*or in my terms the real self*—JFM) and ego identity: personal entity is a conscious feeling based on two simultaneous observations: the perception of the self sameness and continuity of one's existence in time and space and the perception of the fact that others recognize one's sameness and continuity. Ego identity, however, is the quality of that existence in its subjective aspect; it is the awareness of the fact there is a self sameness and continuity to the ego synthesizing methods. (p. 219)

The real self, then, provides an internal repertoire that, although finite and fixed, is varied and flexible enough to blend the need for real self-expression with the external roles required by adaptation.

DEVELOPMENT OF THE REAL SELF

The ingredients or building blocks of the real self consist of the biologic and genetic endowment, the child's experience of proprioceptive and sensory sensations from his or her own body, as well as pleasure in increasing mastery in coping with the environment plus the interactions with a caring object as described by Mahler and McDevitt (1982):

I will assume the infant has two basic points of reference from which he builds up his self schema: one, his own inner feelings or states forming the primitive core of the self on the one hand and, two, his sense of the care given by the libidinal object on the other hand. Insofar as the infant's development of the sense of self takes place in the context of the dependency on the mother, the sense of self that results will bear the imprint of her caregiving. (p. 837)

(I understand this to mean the mother's capacity to acknowledge and respond with support to the unique emerging self.) During symbiosis and the differentiation subphase, the caregiver's mirroring is a most important ingredient in the development of the sense of self.

It is postulated that in the first three months of life, the autistic stage, there exists representationally an undifferentiated matrix. During the next or symbiotic stage (approximately between 3 to

18 months of age), based upon the mother's rewarding and frustrating ministrations, two fused symbiotic self object representations emerge from that matrix. Mahler and McDevitt (1982), elaborated on this as follows:

> Although there are similarities in the manner in which the infant examines the mother's, then later the other's face, visually and by touch, and the way in which he examines and familiarizes himself with his own body, it should be pointed out that during the entire differentiation subphase and under average expectable conditions he appears to have by far greater attention to the mother than to himself. The infant seems to sense that the mother is the one who brings about pleasurable and relieves unpleasurable body feelings. In short, the mother in addition to being a checkpoint for *differentiation* has become indispensable for the infant's sense of *wellbeing*. At 5 to 6 months the infant begins to pay attention to the movement of his fingers, hands and arms as they are reflected in the mirror.
>
> Between 12 and 18 months we found that the infant became increasingly aware that the figure he saw in the mirror was indeed himself. By this time or later when asked he was able to identify the mirror image by using either its name or a personal pronoun or by pointing to his chest. During the practicing subphase from 10 to 15 months the infant's innate maturational pressure towards individuation and autonomy contributed most clearly to his sense of entity and identity.
>
> As the infant explored the animate and inanimate world with all sensory modalities he learned more and more about himself and his relationship to the outside world. How the infant felt about himself during the practicing subphase depended on both subphase adequate mothering and fathering and on his autonomous achievements. If adequate, these experiences created sound secondary narcissism consisting of self-love, a primitive evaluation of his own accomplishments and omnipotence. At the same time, the constructive use of aggression promoted turning passive into active mode thereby enhancing his ability to physically distance the self from objects. That is to say, the achievement of a distinct and separate sense of self. (p. 839)

During the next or separation-individuation phase between 18 and 36 months of age, achievement of the capacity to physically separate from the mother impels the parallel intrapsychic task of separation of the self representation from the object representation which occurs according to the same two parameters seen in the symbiotic phase. The good self separates from the good object, the bad self from the bad object. With further development through the subphases of separation and individuation (differentiation, practicing, rapprochement), the split self and object representations come together in the final subphase on the way to object constancy as a whole self representation both good and bad and a whole object representation both good and bad.

This move has profound consequences for both ego development and the development of the self. As a consequence of this developmental move, the child, through processes of identification and introjection, internalizes the ego functions the mother had performed for him, achieving better reality perception, frustration tolerance, impulse control, and ego boundaries. Repression comes to take the place of splitting as the principal mechanism of defense and the capacity for object constancy begins to develop, i.e., the capacity to perceive and emotionally invest a person as a whole, both good and bad, to retain the investment despite frustration, and to retain the intrapsychic image of the person when absent.

Capacities of the Self

Simultaneously and in parallel with the maturation of ego functions, and with self and object representations becoming whole, the now whole, separate, real self becomes autonomous and takes on its capacities. These capacities were identified clinically mostly by their impairment and repair in borderline and narcissistic patients. This list is probably far from complete but forms an adequate clinical working scheme:

1. *Spontaneity and aliveness of affect.* The capacity to experience affect deeply with liveliness, joy, vigor, excitement and spontaneity.

2. Self-entitlement. From early experiences of mastery coupled with parental acknowledgment and support of the emerging self, the sense builds up that the self is entitled to appropriate experiences of mastery and pleasure, as well as to the environmental input necessary to achieve these objectives. This sense, of course, is sorely deficient in the borderline disorder and pathologically inflated in the narcissistic disorder.

3. Self-activation, assertion and support. The capacity to identify one's unique individuative wishes and to use autonomous initiative and assertion to express them in reality and to support and defend them when under attack.

4. Acknowledgment of self-activation and maintenance of self-esteem. To identify and acknowledge to oneself that one's self (in both senses of the term) has coped with an affective state and/or an environmental issue or interaction in a positive, adaptive manner. This acknowledgment is the vehicle for autonomously fueling adequate self-esteem.

5. Soothing of painful affects. The capacity to autonomously devise means to limit, minimize and soothe painful affects.

6. Continuity of self. The recognition and acknowledgment through an effective supraordinate organization that the I of one experience is continuous over time and related to the I of another experience.

7. Commitment. To commit the self to an objective or a relationship and to persevere, despite obstacles, to attain that goal.

8. Creativity. To use the self to change old, familiar patterns into new, unique and different patterns.

9. Intimacy. The capacity to express the self fully in a close relationship with minimal anxiety about abandonment or engulfment.

Although the self becomes autonomous and able to perform its functions at this point in development, further increments are added during the phallic-oedipal phase, latency and adolescence. Since the developmental arrest of the self in the borderline and narcissistic patients occurs before these latter phases, I will not consider them in detail but only in summary form.

To describe the further development of the real self, one can take the self aspect of Erikson's (1968) concept of self-identity, realizing but putting aside for the moment that his perspective is not intrapsychic but psychosocial. As the child passes through subsequent psychosocial stages, the resolution of each provides certain capacities for the self such as industry, initiative, etc.

The whole process of development of the self culminates in the normal identity crisis of adolescence where:

> In an ever-changing social reality the adolescent must test, se-
> lect and integrate the self images derived from the psychosocial
> crises of childhood in the light of the ideological climate of
> youth. In their search for a new sense of continuity and same-
> ness which must now include sexual maturity, adolescents
> must come to grips again with the crises of earlier years before
> they can extol lasting idols and ideals as guardians of the final
> identity. Identity formation in adolescence arises from the re-
> pudiation and mutual assimilation of childhood identifications
> and their absorption in a new configuration which in turn is
> dependent on the process by which society, often through sub-
> societies, identifies the young individual, recognizes him as
> somebody who had to become the way he is and to be what
> he is is taken for granted. (Erikson, 1968, p. 159)

The final identity or self is fixed at the end of adolescence as superordinate to any single identification with individuals of the past. It includes all significant identifications, but it also alters them in order to make a unique and reasonably coherent whole. The self aspect of this identity emerges from experiences by which temporarily confused selves are successfully reintegrated in an ensemble of roles which also secure social recognition. One could speak of ego identity when one is thinking of the ego's synthesizing power in the light of its central psychosocial function, and of self-image identity when the integration of the individual self and role images is being considered.

Although the ego identity is fixed, the self aspect is not and remains open to further modifications based on inputs later in life.

PARENTAL ACKNOWLEDGMENT AND DEVELOPMENT OF THE REAL SELF

This real self emerges and develops under a combination of nature/nurture forces: a combination of constitutional endowments, genetic biologic pressure, and the mother's and father's capacity to acknowledge, respond and give emotional support to the unique characteristics of the emerging self during those important first three years of life.

This mirroring or matching process seems vital to the development of the real self. It is important to keep in mind that I do not mean physical caretaking such as feeding, clothing, etc., but rather the capacity of the parents to perceive the unique characteristics of the child's emerging self and to respond to these in a positive, supportive manner, to identify, acknowledge and treat with respect his or her unique temperament (Chess, Thomas, & Birch, 1968), to encourage the unique style or manner in which the child's individuation is expressed in his exploring, experimenting, self-assertive adventures with reality. Failures in this parental function make an important contribution to the failure of the self's development and, therefore, to the production of a narcissistic or borderline personality disorder.

CHAPTER IV

The Impaired Real Self:
Psychopathology

INTRODUCTION

The term real self refers to the normal, healthy, intrapsychic self and object representations and their related affects. It functions alongside and with the ego to effectively adapt and defend in order to maintain a continuous source for the autonomous regulation of self-esteem as well as to creatively identify and articulate or express in reality the self's unique or individuative wishes.

In understanding the functioning of the real self, it is important to keep in mind that like its partner, the ego, it is primarily directed toward reality. Erickson's (1968) definition of a strong ego could be applied to the real self. "It utilizes its volition or will to 'test what feels real,' the mastery of that which works, the understanding of that which proves necessary, the enjoyment of the vital, and the overcoming of the morbid." Jahoda's (1950) definition of the healthy personality also would fit the real self: "One which actively masters the environment, shows a certain unity of personality, is able to perceive the world and the self correctly."

For a clinical example of the operation of the real self, consider a young psychologist who submits his first version of his Ph.D. thesis to his advisory committee and is told that in some areas it lacks information and in others the writing is poor.

Since the cornerstone of his real self is his sense of self-entitlement, he feels entitled to mastery and whatever input that this requires, plus his capacities for self-activation, assertion and commitment. He realizes at the outset that the purpose of submitting his thesis at that time was to learn its deficiencies so that he could correct them. He then applies his creativity, commitment and self-assertion to find ways to learn the necessary knowledge and improve his writing. By mastering his reality problem, he has provided an autonomous feedback to support his self-esteem or self-image, a support which also is soundly based on reality.

When we turn to the psychopathology of the self in the borderline and narcissistic personality disorders, we find there is a split between the real self, which is impaired, and the false defensive selves. In addition, the false defensive selves are based on fantasy, not reality, and their principal function is not to cope with reality as such but to defend against painful affect at the cost of reality.

THE DEFENSIVE OR FALSE SELF AND THE IMPAIRED REAL SELF OF THE BORDERLINE PERSONALITY DISORDER

In the borderline personality disorder, all the capacities of the real self are impaired to some degree: to spontaneously activate the self with supportive self-assertion, to acknowledge self-worth and self-activation and mastery, to feel self-entitlement, to be able to soothe intense affects, to identify the self's unique individuated wishes and activate them in reality, to make and pursue a commitment, and to be creative.

Those impaired by this disorder are unable to use the real self to react to reality challenges with supportive, realistic self-assertion, but turn instead to a false defensive self—a product of the alliances between the pathological ego, the rewarding object relations part unit and the withdrawing object relations part unit. This leads to avoidance, passivity, denial, and preoccupation with fantasy, thus further feeding their lack of self-esteem.

Their defensive self representations—based mostly on fantasy rather than reality—consist of two equally unrealistic fantasy images: that of a helpless child who is loved or rewarded for not asserting himself and an inadequate, evil, bad self which impels the mother to withdraw.

Beyond that, there is no sense of unity, wholeness or continuity of self. In other words, there is psychopathology at the level of both subordinate self representations and superordinate self-organization in that the self representations are based mostly on fantasies (derived from the childhood past) and are products of the need to avoid the abandonment depression and the failure to develop. Their purpose is to defend against pain and not to deal with reality. They are intensely fixed, rigid and unable to accommodate a variety of environmental roles.

Parenthetically, all of these symptoms are included in the descriptive list for the borderline in DSM-III (1980) in a general context rather than specifically focused as they are here on the psychopathology of the self.

To extend the metaphor of the psychology student to contrast the operation of the borderline, false defensive self with the real self: Because of his difficulty with self-activation, assertion and commitment, and creativity, the student might procrastinate and delay submitting his thesis way beyond the deadline. The critical comments would be felt as a reinforcement or proof of his inadequate self and would precipitate an abandonment depression to which he would respond by helpless clinging to a teacher or other authority or by avoiding the project altogether. This, of course, would further reinforce his sense of an inadequate self.

CLINICAL EXAMPLES OF THE BORDERLINE PERSONALITY DISORDER: THE FALSE DEFENSIVE SELF AND THE IMPAIRED REAL SELF

The clinical appearance and function of the false defensive self of the borderline personality disorder are enormously varied and subtle. The patient must slowly become aware not only that it is destructive to his real self, but also that he or she has been actively colluding with it.

A young woman dropped out of college and complained of depression, of often being unable to feel at all, of excessive day dreaming, and of binge-overeating and obesity. It was also quite apparent, although she was not aware of it, that she had great difficulty asserting herself and that she let people take advantage of her.

In treatment, confronting how harmful it was to her to give up the assertion of her real self slowly enabled her to begin to assert her real self with her roommate who was criticizing her. As soon as she did, she felt anxious and depressed, immediately cut off all feeling, and again gave up self-assertion: "When it is most important to support myself, it is most difficult. I feel like doing it, I do it, and then immediately I cut off. I am scared to death of that other person, who causes me to give up and wipes me out, who pulls the wool over my eyes. For example, even if I do assert myself, as I did with my roommate, by the time I report it here in the interview something (the defensive self) has taken away the feeling, so there is no feeling. The anger is gone, so it is just empty reporting. The power of the negative force is unreal. When I am abused and taken advantage of, I react passively and then turn and attack myself." Her defensive self functioned by impelling her to give up self-assertion, cut off all feeling, and retreat to daydreaming, and passivity.

A borderline defensive self derived from clinging to others as a form of motivation illustrates well the relationship between the real self and the defensive self. A woman begins to talk about how important it is for her to please other people. She reports being terribly upset about her mother who she thinks may be seriously ill. She calls the mother's doctor and is surprised to hear him report that her mother is not doing that badly. This leads to an awareness that her mother, a martyr, sends the patient messages of suffering to induce her to become the mother's caretaker. She then goes a step further to note that perhaps she complies with her mother in order to avoid her real self: "My mother uses complaints to manipulate me, and I become a good girl and take over for her to avoid my real self. When I have to face my self, I shut down, as I am doing right now in the session."

At the very next session she saw my prior patient leaving the office and remarked sympathetically: "You don't even have a break between patients." She was inviting me to complain. However, I responded, "Why are you thinking about me rather than yourself?" I then pointed out that she was, in essence, inviting me to complain to her the way the mother complained and, thereby, setting herself up again to avoid her real self. She pursued it further by saying that after the last session she realized that when her real self was on center stage, she had shut down all feeling, was anxious about coming to this session, and didn't know what to talk about, i.e., how to activate her real self.

A man had a similar life-style of clinging to others' expectations to motivate his behavior so as to avoid real self expression. After a long struggle in treatment with his defensive self, he reported finally a brief glimpse of getting in touch with his real self as follows: "I had just left an appointment and found I had some free time. I was walking down the street and suddenly realized a feeling of freedom, of being able to do what *I* wanted. When I looked at other people, I really saw them without being concerned about how they were looking at me. I was expressing myself with people, talking to them in the stores as I shopped; the feeling and expression flowed but was within control, and I felt good, good about myself (*spontaneous expression of the real self with a self-image of feeling good*). I felt that the secret of life was in being in touch with your own feelings (real self) and expressing them with others, not worrying so much about how others felt about you." Then the other (*defensive*) self took over. "When I got home I began to eat and couldn't stop. I found I had cut off all feeling—I was disgusted. The latter part is a robot, a computer who takes over whenever I get in touch with my real self."

Another man, in his thirties, spent years in treatment struggling with his depression and his defensive self's destructive behavior: drugs, alcohol and promiscuous sexual behavior. As these symptomatic behaviors subsided and he began to get a perspective on his real self and the defensive self, he reported: "I had a full-blown anxiety attack—terrible dizziness. My fear of having this attack is what motivates that other self (*the defensive self*)—what used to keep me chasing alcohol, drugs or women. I saw it so clearly this weekend. If I take charge of myself (the real self), I will lose this notion of my mother. I would do anything to keep this image of her there. Alcohol, drugs, women. She never let me grow—I always needed her close. I came to believe I couldn't function without her and I get overwhelmed with anxiety. It's hard to believe that at this age I could still have the feelings of an infant. I even get annoyed that I have to take care of myself one hundred percent."

A 30-year-old woman with two children begins to examine the relationship of her real self to the defensive self. "I was not worthy because I didn't have a real self. I was a vampire who lived off other people. So needy. How I deluded myself; how reluctant I was to try my real self out, to even see what's inside. Such a phenomenally strong attachment to my mother. All the years of avoiding my real self for this fantasy about her. I am preoccupied with surfaces. How I look, other people, what they think. It's so hard to deal with my real self. To finally see my real self is to be like a prisoner released after twenty years: Everything seems so alien; I'm afraid of it because I don't have a grip on myself. I find it so frustrating that I can't crawl any more into someone else's skin. I cop out on myself by being the other person. Still, I am unwilling to accept the reality of my real self because it interferes with my old fantasies of being the center of my mother's attention" (*the defensive self*).

A young executive who similarly functioned by clinging to the expectation of others, reported: "I don't do what I want (*express his real self*) because my ideas of what I want are filtered through the perception of what others want: how I think; how I dress; how I work; even my recreation and how I relate to women. I then blame what's wrong on my life-style, on what I am doing rather than on my motivation, on why I am doing it. I am good at perceiving what pleases other people and I give them what they want and pay a terrible price for it. I make changes in my life-style, but it doesn't work. I am like a chameleon—I make changes to suit the expectations of the environment. I have been operating like a robot with expectations of others rather than my real self. On the other hand, all my life I felt (*my real self*) trapped, suffocated and yearned to be free, and I am angry with my self for not having the courage to come out to express itself."

The following case considers the issue of the false defensive self in more detail.

Chief Complaint

Jean (age 17) complained of difficulty managing her weight for the last four years, either "pigging out" and gaining 30 to 40 pounds or drastically dieting. These complaints had increased in severity in the last two years following her sister's marriage. She avoided going to school when overweight because she felt she was so "disgusting," and in the last year she had missed 50 days. She reported being depressed but not suicidal and of being more in conflict with her father than with her mother. Jean had had two years of prior treatment twice a week without any change.

The mother's complaints were: Jean was unmotivated, irresponsible, did not take care of herself, her clothes, or her room, slept all day, demanded the mother's time, was disrespectful, and wanted to be waited on.

The father's complaints were: She was selfish, lazy, demanding, spoiled, did nothing for anyone else, expected to be waited on, and tried to get everything she could out of him.

Past History

Jean was born to an upper middle-class family, the second of three children, with a sister six years older and a brother one year younger who was viewed by the family as "the all-American boy."

The mother recalled Jean as being essentially a "contented and happy baby." When she was 11 months of age, her brother's birth led to temporary loss of bowel control and a retreat to the bottle. She used a pacifier until age three.

Early development was otherwise normal; however, when the parents were questioned about the past history, their memory was unusually vague. She evidently had no difficulty starting school, where she did well and had no problems socially or any later evidence of childhood symptomatology. There was much rivalry between her and her younger brother. There were a number of changes in residence between ages 7 and 15.

Menarche occurred at age 14. There were no menstrual problems. She had had dating relationships with boys but little sexual activity, feeling that boys were "out to get what they could from her." She had just barely graduated high school and was planning to go away to college. Her principal outside interest was singing.

A brief evaluation of the parents showed the father to be narcissistic, angry and demanding. He had been sent to a military school by his father because of stealing and discipline problems. He was very successful in business. The mother's father died when she was six and her mother remarried when she was 13. The mother had graduated high school and shortly after married the father and had two abortions and three children in quick succession. An attractive, compliant woman on the surface, Jean described her as idealizing the father, unable to be physically affectionate, and extremely resentful of the burden of being a mother, particularly of the patient.

Psychiatric Examination

Jean's physical appearance was striking. She looked like a very attractive teenager trying to look like a chorus girl in her mid-twenties: dyed red hair, excessive lipstick and makeup, revealing dress, and spike heels. She was depressed, angry and detached. There was no thinking disorder, and there was adequate and appropriate affect.

She described her prior treatment as follows: "The therapist said at first that my problems were 'normal and not to worry,' so I let go and got worse. Then she told me that I was in conflict with my mother. How could that be when I love my mother?"

Jean would report other people's (mother, father, therapist) opinions about her, but had great trouble describing her own feelings and thoughts. She had no delusion of body image, was able to see herself as both thin and fat, and had no history of vomiting or purging, i.e., she was not anorectic or bulimic.

First Course of Psychotherapy (Three Months)

Jean was seen three times a week by one of my staff throughout the summer. The therapist confronted the patient with the self-destructive and maladaptive aspects of her regressive and avoidant behavior, as well as trying to help her get in touch with her feeling states.

Despite the efforts of a very competent therapist, the patient in essence "stonewalled" the therapy and there was no progress. At the end of the summer, against our emphatic advice that she should continue treatment, she left to follow through on the original plan to go away to college. She managed to get through the first semester, having great trouble with depression, dieting and binging. In the middle of the second semester, she was no longer able to manage because she was again missing classes. She dropped out and returned to see me for consultation.

The prior work had convinced me that Jean's diagnosis was a false-self type of Borderline Personality Disorder and that her pathological defenses had become identified as her self-image and that she would be a difficult treatment case, especially in the light of the two failed attempts. I decided to undertake the treatment myself and as a condition recommended that she should not live at home and should have a job. These environmental arrangements were suggested to deal with two aspects of her psychopathology: to physically remove her from constant contact with negative parental projections and to place her in an environment where she was required to take responsibility for herself, thus providing an obstacle to the operation of her regressive defensive self whose defensive function was to avoid the internal experience of anxiety and depression associated with her real self.

I recognized that this recommendation ran the risk of resonating with her rewarding unit and reinforcing resistance that would have to be dealt with later in the treatment, but felt the risk had to be taken since her regressive environment had played such an important role in defeating previous attempts at therapy.

Psychodynamics and Intrapsychic Structure

In the first few months of treatment, observations about Jean's psychodynamics and intrapsychic structure and the clinical manifestations of her borderline triad and defensive false self made it possible to design a therapeutic plan. It appeared that Jean's defensive false self had arisen partially because she had been the repository or container of the negative projections of both the parents; she was required to process these feelings for the parents in order that they not feel the painful feelings of dependency and guilt. For example, the father, through the process of projective identification, projected his despised dependent self-image upon Jean and saw her as no good, lazy, demanding, doing nothing for herself. Jean, therefore, had to identify with this projection of the father and act lazy, demanding, etc. in order to defend him against his awareness of his own dependency needs.

The mother projected a different set of negatives. An empty, dependent, passive, depressed, compliant borderline woman in great conflict with her narcissistic husband, she felt the deprivation of having to be a mother and take care of these children when she felt so needy, empty and deprived of dependency satisfactions herself. On the one hand, the mother clung to the patient, rewarding her regressive behavior and withdrawing from her individuative behavior to defend against her own depression and to prevent the patient from separating. In addition, the mother projected her guilt and depression onto the patient who was required to contain and process these painful affects. Paradoxically, at the same time, Jean had to play the role of the mother's mother and listen to her problems and try to give her advice.

When Jean was born, the parents, who had badly wanted a boy, were terribly disappointed. When the next child, born 11 months later, was a boy, they demonstrated in the most gross and obvious ways their preference for the all-American boy. A further complication was that both parents were overtly very religious. While verbalizing love for mankind, they were continually neglecting, seducing and attacking Jean's self-expression.

The patient's false defensive self derived from the need to carry the father's negative feelings about his dependency needs and the mother's depression and dependency needs. Jean did this by identifying with these projections and developing a false, defensive self that was a compliant, helpless, dependent little girl. The theme revolved around her own real self-activation or assertion. If she did act in an autonomous or self-activated manner, both mother and father would attack her. In other words, as long as the patient was "bad," the parents could feel "good."

These themes were then internalized or introjected by the patient to form the patient's intrapsychic structure: a rewarding part-unit* consisting of a maternal part-object which the patient experienced as loving caretaking, with a heavy emphasis on reward for regressive, dependent, helpless, clinging behavior. The defensive self representation was of being helpless and clinging; the affect that linked these two was very clearly one of feeling loved based on the mother's verbalizations, not on the reality of her behavior. The withdrawing part-unit** consisted of a part-object representation of an attacking "witch" that was deeply defended against by splitting. The part-self representation was of being nothing, worthless, undeserving, useless. The affect that linked this part-object and part-self representation—abandonment depression—did not emerge until much later in the work and had as its major component a severe separation panic when she was alone or managed herself independently. The other ingredients of the abandonment depression were also present: depression, guilt, helplessness and hopelessness, and massive rage which was also heavily defended against, and an absence of any feeling of self-entitlement.

---

*RORU—Rewarding object relations part-unit.
**WORU—Withdrawing object relations part-unit.

The Borderline Triad

The borderline triad—activation of the real self or individuation leads to depression which leads to defense—operated in the following manner: Jean's behavior was regressed in the sense that she avoided real self-activation or individuation at all costs and functioned through the operations of the defensive self—i.e., compliant behavior with others. The abandonment depression and the separation panic with underlying rage were stimulated whenever: (1) an external situation like going away to college involved separation and required more real self activation; or (2) she tried to activate her real self in her psyche; or (3) she was exposed to a neglectful or seductive experience at the hands of either parent. These separation and individuation stresses would trigger the depression (withdrawing object relations part-unit) which would then trigger a "pigging out" in order to relieve it (rewarding object relations part-unit). Beyond this, and far more significant clinically, was a defensive detachment of affect. The patient would describe herself as feeling nothing at all and being preoccupied mainly with what I would call rewarding part-unit daydreams. Her family referred to her as being a "dizbat" or "dizzy" because of the frequency of these detached states. Teachers in grammar school complained of her "daydreaming."

Through the operation of the splitting defense, she maintained that she had more problems with her father than with her mother despite many episodes of the mother offering material and physical rewards for regressive and clinging behavior. The patient accepted these only to "pig out" later in order to deal with the rage and depression which these seductions impelled.

Plan of Treatment

The treatment plan was to confront the maladaptive or self-destructive aspects of her avoidance of real self activation and the operations of her defensive self: her regressive, clinging and avoiding defenses, and at the same time try to help her overcome the detachment and get in touch with her affective states and how they related to her defensive behavior. She initially described overeating "only when alone, feeling desperate; afterwards feeling furious and hopeless and giving up, feeling her parents had given her everything, how could she be this way?" She would then detach all feeling to enter the daydreaming state. She felt guilty, hopeless, like a leech who had ruined the father's life.

These examples illustrate that one has to try to distinguish between the false defensive selves, whose purpose is defense, and the more underlying difficulty in functioning of the real self. It would appear that the real self representation lies dormant or latent behind or beneath the defensive self and that its reactivation in treatment by the therapist's confrontations brings both the abandonment depression and the difficulties of the real self's functioning to the center stage of treatment.

THE DEFENSIVE OR FALSE SELF AND THE IMPAIRED REAL SELF OF THE NARCISSISTIC PERSONALITY DISORDER

The clinical quality of the intrapsychic fused self-object representation or false defensive self of the narcissistic personality disorder is such that it can confuse the observer—and often the patient as well—as to whether or not it is the real self or a defense against it. Such qualities as the grandiosity of the self representation and the omnipotence of the object representation, together with the free access to aggression and the capacity to maintain almost continuous activation of this fused object relations unit and to deny depression and devalue environmental traumas, permits the narcissistic personality disorder to coerce the environment into resonating with the grandiose self-projection, thereby continually refueling the grandiose self and perpetuating the illusion of its stability. The patient feels grand, like a manic-depressive patient in the manic phase, and this feeling is reinforced by his perception of the world and the world's reinforcing feedback. This also helps to explain how the narcissistic personality disorder, though suffering from developmental arrest of self and ego, nevertheless is better able to express his creativity than the borderline, especially if that creativity is along exhibitionistic lines like in artist, actor, politician, etc. Within his self-contained cocoon of grandiosity and free aggression, his imagination and creativity have free play. Up to a point, his denial of reality supports the self-contained state, although it is obvious that if the denial is too great it will cause conflict. Incidentally, though the narcissistic disorder denies reality to himself, he uses his hypersensitivity to the responses of others in order to manipulate them for his narcissistic purposes.

The creative exhibitionistic act is itself a prime source of gratification, even in narcissistic disorders who are not particularly creative since this form of expression is their unique mode. As a result, the subsequent reinforcement of the gratification from the environment if the product is of true creative value forms a closed circle of seeming reinforcement and stability which again has the illusion of the effectiveness and stability seen in the real self.

The illusory quality of this defensive self is revealed by its content, its motives, and the denial or devaluation of reality required. The content revolves around grandiosity and omnipotence, while the motivation is to seek narcissistic supplies: to be unique, special, adored, perfect in form and function, and to find wealth, power and beauty. Joined to this is the extraordinary denial of the reality of any stimuli that frustrate these projections. As soon as the narcissistic personality disorder in treatment has to step out of his narcissistic cocoon and activate his real self—i.e., to pursue real self expression in reality or real relationships—the underlying difficulty with the functioning of the real self emerges. From an object relations perspective, this is the activation of the fragmented self representation of the underlying aggressive fused self-object representation. Now the narcissistic disorder shows all the difficulties in functioning and feeling listed previously: self-activation, entitlement, continuity, etc.

A narcissistic disorder patient who was transference acting-out by idealizing the therapist maintained that without my help he "couldn't activate himself in the session." He couldn't start the interview, had no spontaneity, couldn't identify and express his thoughts, etc. In my view, he was also unable to acknowledge the effectiveness of his real self when he finally did activate it. His lack of self-entitlement or sense of self-worth was apparent. However, when his grandiose self-projection of perfection was reinforced, either in life or in treatment, he felt fine and was able to activate himself easily and successfully. Small wonder that he was confused as to which was his real self.

In contrast to the defensive self of the borderline patient which is emotionally involved with the therapist in a distorted way, the narcissistic personality disorder is unable to be genuinely emotionally involved. Therefore, one of their principal difficulties with the real self is their inability to emotionally commit themselves to a relationship and involvement because it would activate the underlying emptiness of the impaired real self. This underlying severe impairment in the capacity to be genuinely emotionally involved is camouflaged and hidden by continuous activation of the grandiose self's omnipotent object projections which create the illusion of emotional relatedness.

The patient's sensitivity to narcissistic wounds makes him extremely perceptive of and sensitive to other people's narcissistic needs and he uses this perception to coerce or manipulate them, through gratifying their narcissistic needs, into reinforcing his grandiose self projection. The very real cleverness, charm or charisma possessed by some narcissistic personality disorders can make an extremely convincing illusion of relatedness. The basically narcissistic nature of the interchange, however, becomes apparent whenever the relationship comes upon issues which produce narcissistic disappointment in the patient or which don't bear on his narcissism; he then demonstrates his total lack of concern or interest. Who has not had the social experience with people with narcissistic personality disorders of seeing the apparent interest and warmth with which they respond when they are being asked about themselves. However, they do not ask you about yourself and they manifest an obviously formal attitude towards you, evidently either trying just to conform to social norms or to manipulate you, to maintain you as a narcissistic supply. It is equally interesting to note how, if you stop asking them about themselves, the relationship quickly disintegrates and they find ways to avoid you. You have ceased to exist for them as a source of narcissistic supplies.

To extend the metaphor of the psychology Ph.D. student, if he were a narcissistic disorder he would confidently submit his thesis, anticipating admiration for his perfection. The criticisms would be seen as attacks and would precipitate his underlying aggressive unit with its harsh attacking object and fragmented self. He would defend by either seeing the committee as harsh and unfair or devaluing their ability and right to criticize. The reality of the paper's defects would be denied.

Clinical Example of False Defensive Self and Impaired Real Self of Narcissistic Personality Disorder

Mr. X, 32, who had an overdetermined pathologic identification with his extremely successful, narcissistic mother, came to treatment because of "marital problems," the problem being that his wife, also a narcissistic personality disorder, was not prepared to subordinate herself to the narcissistic activities of the patient and his mother. The patient considered his wife to be one hundred percent wrong.

He described the feeling state of his grandiose self as "supremely confident about myself, in charge of myself and the world but often overstimulated." At the beginning of treatment he had no awareness that this was a false defensive self and that there was a severe impairment of the functioning of his real self, i.e., that he had allowed his real self to languish.

As he attempted to activate his real self in the course of treatment, he became more and more aware of the defensive nature of his grandiose self and considered it to be a "clone" of his mother. However, although he felt good and functioned well in this state, it had produced a number of difficulties both in career and relationships.

His efforts to activate the real self in treatment created extreme difficulty. He couldn't identify his thoughts and feelings, he got terribly sleepy, his memory was blocked, he couldn't remember from session to session.

The operation of his grandiose self was illustrated as follows: Although not currently active as a tennis player, he competed and did poorly in a local tournament. He was very disappointed in himself. On further consideration, he felt that the disappointment was unrealistic; since he hadn't trained, the other players were certainly better equipped and therefore he should not have expected to do well. Nevertheless, he was disappointed. In other words, his grandiose self's striving for perfection had been frustrated. He then went on to report that he enjoyed doing a lot of things but couldn't stick with any of them: tennis, bridge, his business.

I used this to point out to him that he had such difficulty activating his real self that he was unable to do so both in his treatment and in his life because it meant giving up his grandiose self and facing the subsequent anger and depression. Therefore, he couldn't commit himself to an activity and follow through and develop it. He replied that, "My real self-image is all bound up with my clone image of myself and my mother like two octopuses."

He reported his feeling about the impaired real self as, "I'm nobody, an eggshell to be broken. My mother punched a hole in the shell and sucked out the inside. There's nothing there. I feel no directions, I'm drifting like a spaceship. I'm not only afraid if it's activated, I'm sure it will fail. It makes me feel stupid, an idiot, defective." Outside of the grandiose self, "I have layers of self-hate and despise myself. There's nothing inside, no essence."

The therapist's function as a mirroring object for the patient is indicated by the fact that though I start the session on time and he often was late, if I were a few minutes late, he would stand impatiently outside the door waiting to come in, quite annoyed at how I had frustrated him.

He further reported, "I feel trapped. My real self is trapped. It just can't get out. It's like it's in a laundry bag which my mother tied at the top and has her hand on the string." He spoke of being possessed by the spirit of his mother. "My energies have gone to nurture this monster, this clone, rather than to my real self. I used to have a fantasy as a child of being able to walk on water."

In returning to the grandiose self he says, "In order to feel okay, I had to be the best businessman, athlete, lover, etc., best at everything. In sexual relations I was more concerned about how I functioned in the woman's eyes than with my own satisfaction. I had to perform the best there also.

"I put on my perfect self in order to manage people. I am interested in impressing them, not relating to them. Now that I see that this is a false self, I feel like a hypocrite, I'm a phoney. But underneath I feel the real self is nothing, empty, and cannot manage. For example, when I'm in my perfect self, I have no trouble trying to pick up women or seducing them and I feel confident and superior, but when that passes and I'm in my real self, I feel frightened, shy, self-conscious.

"I could never assert my real self to approach a woman and felt that if I did it wouldn't work. I'm terrified of exposing myself to attack or ridicule. But when I'm in the perfect self, I couldn't care less. I'm not only prepared to be attacked by others but to attack others if the objective requires it. Although I do enjoy tennis, what I really like or am interested in is the applause of the multitudes, to be the center of an adoring multitude, to dream the impossible dream and to fulfill it.

"However, I have learned that even 'the perfect jewel' of external experience does nothing but starve my real inner self. When I'm in that perfect self, I am cut off from my real feelings, but it seems to me that I feel overstimulated, high, almost manic. With women I'm never satisfied. They're not attractive enough, they're not smart enough. If they're smart enough, they're not cultured enough."

This case illustrates the quality of the defensive, grandiose self of the narcissistic personality disorder, particularly the charade-like quality of relatedness, the relentless pursuit of perfection and narcissistic supplies, underneath which are the abandonment depression and the profound difficulties with activating the capacities of the real self. As he describes it, the real self lacked spontaneity, self-entitlement, self-assertion, capacities for commitment and creativity, and the capacity to soothe intense affects. In lieu of the latter he turned to drinking, overeating and sexual acting out to soothe his painful affects.

Second Clinical Example

A 38-year-old married successful lawyer with four children came to treatment because his wife of 20 years was leaving him because "She doesn't want to be abused any more." He was in a state of depression, but more of humiliation and rage at the outrageousness of her wish to leave him. "It would be like my hand leaving my wrist. How can my hand leave my wrist? It's part of me." The patient had always treated his wife as a narcissistic object. However, in recent years, as the children became adolescents, she had started her own business which required her to be out of the home a lot. The patient became more and more enraged at her and treated her even more badly. She finally had enough and decided to leave him.

His past history was relevant in that he came from a poor family and his father was often emotionally ill. His mother idealized her son and saw his intellectual abilities as the vehicle to help the family escape their circumstances. The patient recalled being unhappy as a young child until his intellectual abilities achieved success in school, for which his mother rewarded him.

The unhappiness disappeared and he reported, "I made a perfect little machine of my own design that would always work. It would be the perfect life. I tended to set up a life situation that would never be threatened like my mother and father's. I plugged into education in order to avoid feeling. Feelings were unimportant. I became a kind of fact-gathering machine. As I became more and more successful, I became more and more of a machine, felt I was in control of my entire life and my total self-esteem was based on this control. The perfect performance provided an armour of invulnerability." He attended college and law school while living at home and, as he was about to graduate from law school, got married "in order to set up another home so I could devote myself totally to my work."

As he became aware of his inflated sense of entitlement and his self-centeredness, he reported, "I guess I treated my wife like an audience. I wasn't really interested in her needs. I'm the same with other people. I charm them but I don't let myself get involved. As soon as they're out of sight, they're out of mind. I can't really open up and be my real self. My real self is that of a little boy afraid of being mauled and rejected and hiding beneath this invulnerable armour. Rather than relate, I use achievement to get adulation from other people."

As I brought to his attention in his own words, "the vast, grand scale" of his entitlements, he spoke of being terrified of feeling depressed, his underlying feelings of worthlessness, and his awareness that he built his life around entitlement and busyness in order not to face the loneliness and inner emptiness. One of his principal entitlements in life was to have a woman whose sole function was to take care of him and make his life easier—first his mother, then his wife. His only function was to achieve. "At work I can create applause from moment to moment from my co-workers (narcissistic supplies); however, I expect the same at home from my wife and children. I can recall feeling as a kid I was going to invent a more intricate airtight entitlement machine than either of my parents so that I wouldn't feel humiliated and dependent as they seemed to. Entitlements are my self-image. Without them I will fall apart and feel alone, humiliated, abandoned, not connected. I'm just a big entitlement machine. I think I recognized early that my wife as a person wouldn't fit this big E, so I ignored her."

After his wife left and he had to find a place of his own, he felt more angry, empty, impoverished, and depressed. He had trouble being on time for interviews and trouble concentrating. He said, "I had this insane notion that everybody and everything should flow to me. The idea of a task that doesn't feed my entitlement is impossible. You see I just don't want to do it. In my contempt for myself, I feel reduced, diminished, emasculated. I'm just waiting for magic, I can't confront the reality that I am on my own. My wife was part of myself. I can't say goodbye. It's the price I pay for having lived in fantasy. It was not worth it unless my entitlements can be magically restored. This can't have happened to me. I'm thrown into the water but if I close my eyes I won't be wet and yet I'm soaked.

"I'm furious and enraged at your matter of factness while here

I am bleeding and nobody is rescuing me. There is no magic. It is humiliating. If I can't have the past back I will do nothing. I will not lift these blinders.

"I am whole only by union with another person. Separation makes me empty and collapsed. The bargain was, you take care of me and I won't become me. The loss unmasks what I have tried to keep hidden all my life—my unwillingness to take responsibility for myself (*real self*). I've always been terrified of being on my own which means being alone, feeling naked and vulnerable without entitlements. I'm afraid that without the dream, without the perfection machine, I have no capacities. What tied me together, gave me discipline and grit, was the dream, the entitlement dream. I feel like I'm walking through a movie set as an extra where I had once been the star. I didn't need intimacy from my wife. It was only when she began to frustrate my entitlements that I grew angry and withdrew. I feel I have no resources to operate on my own; I'm shy, unworthy, dependent."

As he separated from the wife and began to build a new life, he started dating and became more aware of his narcissistic entitlement with other women. "I'm seeing this girl and realized that I want her to do what I want. When I want to talk, I want her to listen. I want to have sex when I want it and not when she wants it. I find myself losing interest in her conversation and in her interests. Is this because we don't have anything in common or is it because I expect too much? Am I only attracted sexually to women who see me as a king or a potentate, who belong to me and who I can control and have sex with whenever I want? In other words, they acknowledge my entitlement machine. I pretend that I might care about them. As soon as I'm interested in a woman, she is to amend her life completely to suit mine."

PSYCHIATRIC EXAMINATION OF THE SELF

To clinically evaluate the adequacy of the patient's self, one observes the following: (1) the patient's report of his self and object representations and observation of how he manifests them in the session: whether they are part or whole, good, bad, o:

contradictory, their relationship to reality or fantasy, the degree of unity or wholeness or continuity; (2) his capacity to autonomously regulate self-esteem; (3) the capacity to identify his own wishes, thoughts and feelings and to assert them in reality; (4) the capacities for spontaneity, initiative, involvement, autonomy, creativity.

These observations can be checked and corroborated in the patient's past history of the emergence and functioning of his real self. It makes its central appearance probably between two and three with the toddler's freedom to say no to mother's expectations. As the child grows, it becomes consolidated and manifests itself both in his or her feeling about the self—i.e., self-image—and also in the style or manner in which the patient deals with life—i.e., relationships, school, activities, etc. Does the patient feel confident enough about the real self to identify what he or she wants and experiment with reality to fulfill it?

In this chapter, the underlying impairment of the functions of the real self that lies beneath the defenses and the abandonment depression of the Borderline and Narcissistic Personality Disorders have been described. The following chapter considers treatment of that impairment.

CHAPTER V

Treatment of the Impaired Real Self: Communicative Matching

THERAPEUTIC NEUTRALITY AND OBJECTIVITY

The concept of therapeutic emotional neutrality and objectivity—the therapist's efforts to maintain a neutral and objective attitude to the patient and not become personally involved—arose in psychoanalysis out of an effort to provide a neutral reality screen in the relationship which could be used as a framework against which to identify, contrast, compare and work through the patient's transference projections. This aspect of the therapeutic relationship is called the therapeutic alliance—a real object relationship in which there is a consensus between patient and therapist as to the objective of their work: to help the patient get better through insight, control, etc.

The neurotic patient, with a well-developed autonomous self and a strong ego, has a good capacity to perceive, accept and use the neutrality of the therapist and the therapeutic alliance as a screen against which to measure and understand his projections.

He and his therapist share a common perception and understanding of the reality of the relationship. However, borderline and narcissistic personality disorder patients with their defensive selves and poorly developed egos live in a world bounded by their projections so that the establishing and maintaining of the therapeutic alliance based on the therapist's emotional neutrality is an initial and continuing goal of the treatment.

The poorer reality perception of these patients suggests that maintaining therapeutic neutrality is even more important than with neurotic patients. Their experience in treatment is probably the only place in life where they have the opportunity to be with someone who can remain objective and treat them according to their best therapeutic interests. Therefore, the therapist's neutrality and objectivity become a life preserver for the patient against his projections.

If the therapist alters this stance and becomes personally involved with the patient or steps into the reality of the patient's life, he loses the objectivity of his perception and judgment and, therefore, his most valuable tool to help the patient. In addition, of course, he resonates with the patient's regressive projections and reinforces resistance. The confrontation of these projections helps the patient to contain them, which allows the emergence of their childhood source in memories, fantasies and dreams. Control of the transference acting-out promotes working through.

To summarize, the therapist behaves in as neutral a manner as possible to provide a setting or condition which offers as little fodder for resonating with the patient's defenses as possible so that the analysis can proceed. The therapist tries to understand and screen out his own countertransference emotions—those that have more to do with his personal past than with his treatment of the patient. He tries to avoid responses that might jeopardize therapeutic neutrality—for example, by reflecting rather than reacting to the patient's angers, fears, depression, and also by not offering personal information.

The vital importance of therapeutic neutrality to the success of the work has led to a distorted, rigidly overdetermined view on the part of some therapists that the therapist somehow must behave like an inhuman block of wood lest he threaten therapeutic neutrality. A parallel view to this attitude is that the *only* therapeutic force in the work is the analysis and working through of the past.

This view overlooks the fact that the structure of the treatment itself provides enormous, positive support and is a powerful therapeutic aid in that it potentiates and creates the conditions for the analytic work. By structure I mean the therapist's implicit assumption that the patient will always act in a mature and adaptive self-interested manner which serves as both a role model for identification and a platform for investigation.

Beyond that, the therapist's emotional calm, together with his attitude of curiosity and investigation amidst the patient's affective storm of hopelessness and helplessness, implicitly conveys a confidence that the patient has the capacity to manage his or her conflicts. This has a soothing effect and encourages the patient to persist with the struggle. For example, a therapist reported in supervision that when her borderline patient's defenses were confronted and the patient had to face and experience her abandonment depression, she dissolved in hopelessness and helplessness, saying she was "up against a wall, could go no further." This precipitated a Rescue Fantasy countertransference reaction in the therapist who felt she had to intervene to get the patient through the wall. The more she intervened, the more helpless the patient became. When the supervisor identified the countertransference and the therapist controlled it and, instead of taking over for the patient, quietly began to investigate the source of the patient's hopelessness, the patient slowly began to face and deal with her depression.

More support is created by the regularity of the sessions, both in frequency and length, and by the therapist's interest in the patient's problem. I say problem because the therapist, if his work is well-motivated, will naturally be interested in the patient's problem. This does not mean that he personally cares about the patient as many borderline patients wish for and insist on. If the therapist were to be personally involved with each patient, he would not only cease to be a therapist but he would be emotionally exhausted.

The accuracy of the therapist's observations and interventions and their usefulness to the patient are both supportive and analytic. For many of these patients, this is the *first* time in their lives that any human being has perceived, acknowledged and responded to their emotional needs in terms of their best interest. By monitoring what the patient can handle emotionally at any given point and limiting his or her interventions accordingly, the therapist can provide the most support. In addition, the interview is an opportunity to express and discharge painful emotions, to review and critique efforts to solve adaptive problems, and to rehearse new adaptive solutions. All of this adds to the therapy by providing an emotional soothing process. Properly managed, these forces make their own positive therapeutic contribution to the work without inducing regressions.

When we shift our focus from all patients to borderline and narcissistic patients, we can say that these positive elements carry even more weight. In addition, the therapist must be a real object or person, not in the sense of sharing his personal life but rather by manifesting an emotionally warm interest in the patient's problems, sympathizing with his real life defeats and congratulating him on his triumphs, and being emphatic about the fact that coping and adaptation are vital to emotional survival. Finally, the therapist serves as an auxiliary ego through his confrontations.

From the point of view of ego psychology and object relations theory, this approach has been necessary to deal with the patient's psychopathology in self and object representations and his ego defects and defense mechanisms. It provided a real object to contend with the patient's intense transference acting-out projections and confrontations to deal with the ego defects and primitive defenses. At the same time, from the point of view of the real self, the patient has experienced all of these therapeutic activities as positive input for his latent embryonic and poorly developed real self.

All of these positive supportive elements have been inherent in the treatment of borderline and narcissistic patients for a long time. Far from causing regression or interfering with the progression of the analytic work, they have provided the conditions which have made analytic work possible (Masterson, 1976, 1981, 1983).

I have described in detail elsewhere the importance of being a real object and an auxiliary ego for the patient while at the same time paying very careful attention to the management of what I call the factors involved in the "frame" of the treatment so as not to resonate with patients' projections—either the rewarding unit or the withdrawing unit—and to avoid producing regressive resistance. By frame factors I mean all those policies around the concrete interactions of the therapy: time, length of interview, fees, phone calls, vacations, lateness, absences, emergencies, etc. The patient must be required to be responsible for his commitment to the treatment and for identifying and reporting his feelings in the interview. This helps to contain the tidal wave of regressive pull of the patient's defensive self—i.e., his transference acting-out.

TREATMENT OF THE IMPAIRED REAL SELF: COMMUNICATIVE MATCHING

The evidence from child observation studies seems clear that in infancy the emergence of the real self from the symbiotic self-object representation to become separate and autonomous and take on its functions requires acknowledgment and support from the mother initially and then also from the father. Again, I do not mean caretaking, i.e., feeding and clothing, but rather the identification and acknowledgment of the child's unique self in its representational and functional aspects and encouragement of its self-assertive and supportive functions. The key is the degree of congruity or harmony between the qualities of the child's emerging self and the mother's capacity to perceive and acknowledge these qualities so that they become consolidated with minimal conflict. Without this crucial environmental input the self does not fully develop its capacities.

This observation that environmental acknowledgment was necessary for development of the self in infancy became reinforced in clinical work with borderline and narcissistic patients where I noted that—despite the fact that much abandonment depression had been worked through—the patient's real self continued to be impaired in that self-activation continued to precipitate depression which was not now relieved by interpretation of the abandonment depression. In other words, although the anchor of the abandonment depression was for the most part removed and despite the presence of the aforementioned positive supportive element in the therapy, the real self did not easily emerge to assume its functions. Something else seemed to be called for. Incidentally, if one accepts Erikson's psychosocial (rather than the intrapsychic) theoretical perspective, an argument could be made that a healthy sense of self-identity and ego identity are always dependent not only on acknowledgment during the developmental years but on a continuing dialogue of acknowledgment with the environment during the rest of life.

As I pondered the problem of what additional therapeutic intervention might be required, I reread Mahler's study of normal separation (1975), focusing this time on the development of the self. I was struck by her description of the toddler's self-assertive explorations of the environment, his return to the mother to present her with nonverbal cues for support, and her providing the nonverbal support which refueled the self-assertive exploration of the environment. She and her workers called this process "refueling." Two issues seem to be condensed in the refueling: (1) providing the child with the required feeling of closeness and acceptance, and (2) also providing emotional acknowledgment and support for the child's unfolding real self as seen in his or her self-assertive explorations. This is demonstrated dramatically in the rapprochement phase when the child repetitively piles all his new toys in his mother's lap for her acknowledgment.

Comparing this scenario of normal development of the real self with the glaring defects of acknowledgment that borderline and narcissistic patients experienced as children led me to the thought that some therapeutic intervention along these lines might provide the "something else" that seemed to be called for.

Communicative Matching

I returned to the clinical situation at the point where the patient had reached that crucial juncture in treatment, i.e., when the abandonment depression had been attenuated and the difficulties with self-activation emerged (patients were usually exploring a new interest, i.e., self-activation or individuation). I now stopped interpreting the abandonment depression and began to discuss with the patient—to share or provide a form of communicative matching with—the reality aspects of this new interest, providing a form of communicative matching by sharing whatever I might know about it and making a particular point of including, if possible, in my remarks some "lessons in life" about how effective adaptation works.

The developmental arrest of the ego, with its ego defects and primitive mechanisms of defense, functions at the cost of reality perception. It is as if this part of the patient's personality had been left in the closet, locked away from learning contact with the environmental stimuli. Meanwhile, the rest of the patient's personality grew—i.e., his body, his intellect, his social behavior; though still dominated by the developmental arrest, these aspects had more adaptive capacity.

The therapist deals with this immaturity by providing a learning experience through his communicative matching responses which are often also confrontations. They may seem obvious and commonsensical to the average mature adult reader because he has learned them from experience and incorporated them in his psyche; they are now an automatic part of his adaptive repertoire. However, these responses are not obvious to the patient. They involve such commonsense notions as:

Work

1. The more work fits what you want, the better it will work and the more you will enjoy it.
2. Experiments are necessary to find what you want.
3. Successful work requires initiative, self-assertion, repetitive effort, honing and refining, picking up after failures, learning from mistakes, and trying again.

Relationships

1. It takes time and experiment to establish a good relationship.

2. The reality of the other person's personality must be tested out and the degree of natural fit determined.
3. The degree of emotional involvement should be titrated to the responses to the experiment.
4. The closer the relationship, the more caution, time and experiment should be used.
5. One has to mourn the end of one close relationship before being able to undertake another.

The patients experienced these interventions as an acknowledgment and refueling of their real self and would then pursue the new interest with persistence, continuity and equally important, a new sense of spontaneity, entitlement and vigor. The real self was overcoming the difficulties and assuming its capacities. These interventions seemed to have done the job. I called this type of intervention communicative matching directed at acknowledging the real self to enable it to overcome its impairment and assume its capacities. Further study of the problem of real self activation revealed that the need for communicative matching actually occurs much earlier in the treatment.

At the outset of treatment the patient, relying on his defensive self, avoids real-self activation, denying the price he pays in reality for this avoidance. The therapist confronts the borderline patient's defensive self and interprets the defensive self of the narcissistic personality disorder as a defense against the abandonment depression. The reality price of the avoidance of real-self activation becomes apparent to both and impels them toward efforts at self-activation which immediately encounters the abandonment depression and the underlying difficulty with real-self activation. For example, there may be difficulty with initiating the interview, actively identifying thoughts and feelings, maintaining a continuity of identification of themes, maintaining involvement and continuity with the therapist, soothing painful affects or regulating self esteem.

In the process of rediscovering his rudimentary capacity for self-assertion to serve as an adaptive guide, each patient struggles to learn to identify his real individuative wishes and articulate

them in the reality of his life; to identify what activities and relationships are unique to his self, reflect mastery and coping, and
build self-esteem so as to begin again his search for a real self.
Thus, efforts to overcome the difficulty with real-self expression
go hand in hand with working through the depression. Each
patient usually selects on his own an activity as a vehicle to facilitate this development. Often these ideas were present years
before, but were not acted on at the time and have lain dormant
since. They represent the reactivation in therapy of unique, individuative wishes and fantasies that were a product of the early
interaction between the embryonal, emerging real self and the
environment. However, they were never activated, or were only
abortively activated because the real self could not assume its
capacities. In addition, there is also the emergence of new wishes
and fantasies.

These ideas and activities have two important characteristics:
1) the patient feels they express his or her own unique real self;
2) they involve turning a passive mode into an active self assertive
one. For example, one patient took up marathon running and
another law, a third, biology, another, medicine. Some chose
more specifically creative activities like writing or acting.

These activities then become the vehicle of the real self to overcome the abandonment depression and its own impaired capacities. This vehicle clarifies the identification of the struggle
between the real self and the borderline and narcissistic defensive
selves. The patient's efforts at self-activation meet success, which
is followed by depression at the temporary surrender of the defensive self, followed by reactivation of the defensive self.

The patient is giving up his defensive self and activating his
real self. It is at this point that the therapist should introduce his
communicative matching interventions, carefully matching them
to fit the vacillations of the patient's attempts at real-self activation. It is extremely important not to get ahead of the patient by
initiating and directing this self-activation as this will become directive and regressive. Let me emphasize again, this is not a license to become a cheerleader for the patient's real self. The
therapist must be sure he is responding to the patient's initiative.

A therapist cannot direct, force, seduce or intimidate real-self activation. The therapist can only create the conditions that make it possible for the patient to activate his real self. If it is going to happen, the patient must take it from there on his own.

How does the communicative matching work? The patient internalizes the therapist as a new positive object representation along with his positive, supportive attitude to the patient's individuation and self representation of being adequate based on self-assertive efforts at adaptation. This new object relations part unit provides the patient with autonomous support for his individuation based on self-assertion, not regression, and serves as a slowly growing buffer against the withdrawing object relations part unit as the patient works through his depression.

It is remarkable with what renewed enthusiasm and vigor the patient resumes his individuative quest once it has been shared with the therapist. As the patient's real self emerges, as seen in the adaptive expression of his real self, the therapist gradually allows the communicative matching interventions to tail off as he sees their internalization in the form of a continuous function of the capacities of the patient's real self. The communicative matching is no longer necessary and would again become regressive.

It is important to keep in mind that the objective of the communicative matching is to help the patient with the quality of what he feels—i.e., spontaneity, enthusiasm, excitement, vigor—as much as with what he does—i.e., self-assertive, supportive adaptive efforts.

There is a second type of empathic communicative matching which comes under the heading that a triumph shared is doubled and a defeat shared is halved. I am referring here to the real life vicissitudes of the patient's efforts at real-self activation. For example, a male patient verbalized his frustration at being caught in the constant struggle between his wife and daughter, with very little power to resolve the conflict. It was not helplessness on his part but an inevitable consequence of his being the father: one of those life situations one has to endure. To emphasize that point and to empathize with his feeling state, I told him the joke of the man who was constantly caught between his mistress and his wife. His friends asked, "How does he always get into these situations?" One friend replied, "Well, he's just lucky I guess."

Another male patient, after a long struggle, is taking over his father's business because of the father's inadequacy. The patient has to do it but feels a great deal of castration anxiety. He had been an admirer of President Kennedy, so to support his self-activation and to decrease his anxiety I remarked that it seemed that in the business the torch was being passed to a new generation. Another patient, a student of Shakespeare, had been so badly damaged by the destructive envy of his peers at work because of his evident superior ability that, disappointed and frustrated, he decided to change jobs. I reminded him of Julius Caesar whose superior abilities also had evoked destructive envy.

Another example is that of men and women who, as a defense against intimacy, pick an unavailable partner to carry out an affair only to be chagrined, astonished and terribly disappointed when the reality of the partner's unavailability can no longer be denied and the affair has to end. They feel depressed, disillusioned, defeated, and angry at all mankind. I tell them the following incident from the movie *A Touch of Class*. The heroine began an affair with an unavailable married man through a chance sharing of a taxi. The affair ends in disappointment. Then, she again shares a cab with a man who is interested in her. However, this time, having learned from her experience, she refuses his overture.

These communicative matching interventions must be properly timed to the patient's clinical needs. Ideally, they should not be used unless there is a firm therapeutic alliance and the patient is actively taking responsibility for his self and working on his abandonment depression. If they are done when the patient is in a regressive, defensive, acting-out stage, they will further regression. To avoid producing a regressive affect from these interventions, one must check the patient's clinical response to them. If the interventions are appropriate, the patient will integrate them, which will lead to more self-activation which will lead to more anxiety and depression. If this does not happen, then the therapist should check for an overlooked defensive state on the part of the patient.

The theoretical base for this therapeutic intervention is that the real self will not emerge and fully assume its capacities without acknowledgment from the environment. Failure to be acknowledged had a great deal to do with its impairment in early development and the therapist's intervention in treatment helps to overcome the impairment.

Is this a form of reparenting, i.e., meeting the patient's deprived infantile emotional needs in treatment? On the surface it would appear that that is exactly what is being done, but more careful study reveals that this is not the case. The issue turns upon the reality of the therapist and his actions versus how the patient experiences them. The therapist is not a parent; he is carefully introducing a therapeutic technique which meets patients' therapeutic needs. The patient, on the other hand, through the transference, particularly his fantasy that the therapist *is* that mother who approves and acknowledges his emerging self that he always wished for, would experience the activity as an effort to substitute or make up for that which he was deprived of in childhood. The difference, then, is between the reality of the therapist and his actions and how the patient perceives and experiences them. This distinction often does not become clear to the patient until the last or separation phase of treatment when the transference fantasy must be analyzed if the patient is to fully resolve his developmental arrest.

A second argument has to do with the fact that this form of intervention may be directive, take over for the patient, and thereby trigger his rewarding unit and become regressive. If the communicative matching is done too early or to excess, is not properly timed and properly dosed, or is continued too long, it will inevitably lead to resistance and regression. The proof of this would be that the intervention would not be integrated, the self would not become more activated, and the patient would not become more anxious and depressed. Similar to the therapeutic technique of confrontation, the basic thrust of communicative matching is towards reality and growth in these particular patients. If they internalize it, they inevitably turn more towards growth, development and reality.

At the risk of becoming repetitive, let me again stress that the therapeutic technique of communicative matching must be used carefully and selectively in combination with the other techniques. It is not an excuse to become an omnipotent guru and try to direct or take over the patient's responsibility for his life.

COMMUNICATIVE MATCHING WITH THE IMPAIRED SELF OF THE BORDERLINE PERSONALITY DISORDER

The following examples illustrate the use of the communicative matching therapeutic technique to help the impaired real self. I shall include only tangentially the material relating to the working through of the abandonment depression, as that has been presented in detail elsewhere (Masterson, 1976). The reader, however, should keep in mind that the working through of the abandonment depression and the activation of the real self go hand in hand. The reader should also keep in mind that this condensation of the clinical material distorts the therapist's role in that it makes him appear more active than would be the case if the complete clinical picture were presented.

Clinical Example: Michael

Michael, a writer with a depression, had had two periods of analysis based on a defensive borderline self, the first in his twenties. There was little improvement. The clinical defensive self of this patient was seemingly airtight and highly intellectualized. He had so completely identified with parental expectations that he saw this defensive behavior as his real self. The motivations and affect of his real self were experienced as a threat producing separation anxiety.

The negative and hostile attacking attitude of his defenses toward his real-self expression emerged in his writing. This had been mostly journalistic and reportorial, but as a first evidence of the activation of his real self, he developed the idea of doing a biography of a historical figure. I happened to have read a lot about this person and, identifying his ideas as the emergence of his real self, I began communicative matching by discussing his ideas for the book in detail, adding a number of my own thoughts about his subject.

He mentioned that I seemed to have a positive attitude toward what he wanted to do, which helped him cope with his own negative self-image. He subsequently had a dream in which he was in a strange city; he felt free, he could be on his own, set his own hours, be unhurried and unpressured. His associations were: "It's the opposite of my pressured life. It's the ability to be free and on my own, but I feel that free time is bad news and will get me into trouble.

"This whole idea of real-self expression, being free, it's like opening the gates of a prison. I feel I'm afraid I'll go out of control. It's succumbing to my own wishes." The patient's extensive identification with the defensive self had impelled him to see his real self-activation as evil, wrong.

He continued to talk about how he saw fun—i.e., the excitement, aliveness, vigor of the real self—as danger. He realized that he was both jailer and prisoner, that he kept himself under tight control because letting go the spontaneity of the real self brought out such enormous anxiety.

He then used the analogy that he was a toiler or laborer in life. He did what was expected. The other option was to be wild, out of control, i.e., his real self. I questioned: "What about the man who has all these potentials but hones them and disciplines them in a sublimated way?"

He reported that many of the so-called choices he had made in his life were not free choices; they did not represent the operation of the real self at all, but were the result of what was expected. Underneath, he resented the work of college and graduate school yet, once he got into the profession, he again did what was expected to "get ahead," rather than what he wanted to do.

A consequence of this form of adaptation—avoidance of real self-activation—was that his life was not providing the gratification and pleasure he had hoped to find. He blamed this on "the way life was" rather than on his own avoidance of real-self activation.

In the next session he detailed his difficulties activating his real self with the biography (avoidance). He procrastinated, wandered about the house, sharpened pencils, ran errands, did anything to avoid getting down to work. When he did start, his mind would wander, he was easily distracted, and he had difficulty pursuing a thought or committing himself to the activation of his real self. He was discouraged and quickly gave up the effort.

However, along with the confrontation of his avoidance and the interpretation of its source, I also continued the communicative matching with further discussions regarding the subject of the biography, managing to get across the idea that successful artistic endeavor requires effort. I cited Balzac, who wrote the first page of each chapter 25 times, or Rodin, who did a hundred studies before embarking on a sculpture. I also described some of my own writing experiences to emphasize the need for effort and perseverance.

He renewed his efforts to write and returned to report some success, asking: "What am I so terrified of?" He then reported memories of his fouling up because of his fear of putting himself on the line (committing his real self) which left him feeling sad about any achievement. He felt small, thin, poor, insignificant.

Some modest satisfaction of his real self in writing led him to become aware that his work schedule was filled with obsessive detail based on fulfilling obligations rather than on what he wanted to do. He began efforts to change. He became aware for the first time of reading from curiosity and interest (the real self) rather than from obligation. From time to time I would discuss the content of his reading with him, in history, sports, literature. He reported: "Life has all been a matter of homework; education for me was a smoke screen to hide avoidance of commitment to my real self. I'm excited about doing what I want to do. I feel real honest-to-God pleasure but another part of me won't give in; there is a break on it and I'm afraid to believe in it, afraid a disaster will occur." After a number of months, as his depression was being worked through and his self-activation increased, he reported for the first time a change in his affect regarding self-activation. He was beginning to enjoy it.

He reported: "Looking back on my life, I see that my lack of confidence in my real self led me to avoid taking risks, feeling pessimistic, dissatisfied and unhappy.

I pointed out that his defensive self seemed to exclude reality entirely; that if he asserted his real self, he considered no consequence other than disaster. I pointed out that even though the treatment had been going fairly well and his writing was improving, he still withheld full commitment to both. He responded: "Whatever I do will turn out badly. I limp through life, avoiding activities, not supporting myself, my own ideas. I'm constantly self-critical, but I'm moving toward a new alignment. I have more confidence in myself, yet I can see myself slip back into it. It is because of the doom and gloom projections."

Occasionally, his real self-activation would shine through these negative projections: "The thought of being able to do what I want *(real self)* is exhilarating to me but makes me anxious. I constantly subject my own ideas *(real self)* to whatever objections or criticisms I raise and then give up. I'm afraid to run my own life. As I begin to change my own schedule and do more of what I want *(real self)*, it's much more enjoyable, but I can't seem to face the world on my own. I give up and go back to holding on *(defensive self)*. Whenever I was away from home, I was happier, but I always went back. I always took the line of least resistance and let other people take over. I was always intimidated and awed by authorities. I have to start taking charge and do what I want *(real self)*. It's such hard work."

I pointed out to him that his attitude toward work was like that of a prisoner on a rock pile, whereas what he actually was considering doing was exactly what he wanted. A short while later he reported: "I can now see my way clear to doing what I want *(real self)*. I have never been so clear about my own projections and my own avoidance. Things are falling into place mostly around my work, and I feel more in control of my life than I ever have. I am amazed at my self-deceptions." This is an awareness every successfully treated patient finally achieves.

Let us now turn to look at Michael three years later, with treatment well on the way to resolving his depression and defensive self and allowing the emergence of his real self, particularly in the area of work. At this point the biography was well on its way, his impaired real self had been for the most part overcome, and he was able to activate his real self and experience pleasure in doing so:

I am now writing twenty hours a week or more. There is no more procrastination. I'm having no difficulty writing; I am enjoying it. It comes very easily, it's smooth, all the difficulty is gone. Where did I get the notion that I couldn't do it? The distorted views I had about myself are amazing. What I want to do with my life in addition is more clearly up to me now than three months ago. I realize I have much more ability. I am much more disciplined now than I was. The problem was not the capacities of myself. The problem was the giving up and giving in (*the defensive self*). I'm getting great pleasure from writing this biography, but the voice in my head says I shouldn't be doing this, I should be doing the conventional thing. What I want to do battles the voice. I feel that if I could let myself go, I could have a lot of fun and do very well with my very good abilities (*real self*). But the voice wants to back me into a secure channel. It constantly attacks my real self growing and blossoming. I'm afraid to even think or dream about what I want. The break is always there, and the voice is so imaginative and persistent. I think my parents installed the voice as a governor to limit myself. No treatment could do any good until I understood the voice and saw that it was running me, that I was an automaton. To suddenly see that so much is possible for me that was denied all these years—that it is all there and possible—is utterly amazing and overwhelming. I know I'll finish the book, I know it will be good and a success. It's incredible to know that the voice prevented me from doing this, even took over my real self image. I didn't know or understand that there was anything else. I feel as if I've been reprieved from a lifelong sentence. I had been sinking in hopelessness and despair. I guess I'm so surprised by the abilities of my real self because the voice kept me from being aware of them. What a relief!

Clinical Example: George

For a second example, let us turn to George, the young executive briefly described on page 35. Like the preceding patient, he also had a borderline false self in that he had identified the behaviors based upon meeting the expectations of the object and the environment as his real self. Keeping in mind that he was working through his abandonment depression at the same time as his real self was emerging, let us now look at how he experienced and expressed the problem.

As George turned from his defensive self to the real self, he began to have difficulty getting to interviews, being on time for interviews, concentrating on thoughts and feelings in sessions. He reported that it was difficult or impossible for him to concentrate on what he was seeing and feeling without being aware of me. He raised the question, "Do I have the courage to deal with the pain? Do I have the courage to throw away the crutches that have kept me together this long? I took charge of myself last night, did not go chasing after women, but was tempted to take drugs. When I take responsibility for myself, I feel frightened and depressed and these harsh voices come in questioning me about not doing it, questioning it, attacking, telling me not to open up to you."

I used here a communicative matching technique to reinforce a confrontation. First I confronted: If he got depressed and anxious because he was activating himself and then took drugs to relieve these feelings, he would only be interfering with his own objective in treatment. Then I compared it with the myth of Sisyphus who eternally rolled a stone up the hill only to let go near the top; it rolled all the way down, and he then had to start again from the bottom. He reported further efforts to activate his real self. "I have difficulty focusing on myself in the interview, the numbness that I feel is awful. Why do I have to deal with this? When I look inside, it's so empty."

George complained constantly of being tired, of being run down, of having no direction. A paralysis of will. He had anxiety about setting limits with his subordinates at work. I again attempted communicative matching, telling him the story of another patient who had been the president of his company. Because of his fear of his board's rejection, rather than make his own decisions and look for the board to ratify them, he turned the decisions over to the board who then, of course, used that to exercise authority over him and discourage initiative.

He had difficulty thinking for himself rather than in the framework provided by others. He had always been ridiculed in his family for thinking for himself and, when he tried to do it with me, he developed anxiety about my approval, fearing that I would attack his independent thinking as his family had.

In a period of long silence he said in a frustrated manner: "I want to express my real self here, to think and talk for myself, but I don't know how. I'm sick and tired of not being able to know what I want. Everything I do is for somebody else. I want to have a life that's my own. I've been operating like a robot, a high paid slave."

He developed urges to write, an interest in music or acting, but none of these were activated. He thought about going into politics but he recognized it was not to express his own political point of view but rather to extend to a larger multitude his need to please the object.

Over several years in treatment, four times a week, as he worked through the defensive self and aspects of the abandonment depression, he gradually got a clearer and clearer perception of the defensive quality of the defensive self, and his real self began to emerge. He stopped almost completely the defensive activities of taking drugs, drinking, dating unavailable women, and excessive busyness.

He said, "I want to throw away any crutch that enables me to avoid my self. I want to support my spiritual side rather than all those material things I had been doing." At this turning point of his treatment, the change was catalyzed by his reading Carl Sandberg's *Lincoln*. He was extremely affected and impressed by Lincoln's secure sense of a real self, his command and control of himself, his immuneness to the expectations of others, and his firm sense of direction. This inspired the patient and he decided,

"I wanted to take charge of myself." This resulted in a dramatic change in his lifestyle. He lived alone in his own apartment and bought a dog which, needless to say, he named Lincoln. This was his first commitment to take care of some object other than himself; of course, he had taken care of himself not in a realistic manner but in a self-indulgent, regressive way. He also had had full-time help to do the cooking and cleaning. He let them go and decided he would do his own cooking and cleaning. He had been overweight so he went on a diet and began to exercise regularly, running and swimming. He took up periods of meditation during the day and decided he would just have to accept the anxiety and depression that went with this kind of change. These activities all illustrated the real self emerging and taking over from the defensive self, an important clinical sign that the treatment was working.

I accompanied these real-self activities with communicative matching: discussing the various kinds of cooking, the intricacies and problems of diets, the important considerations in the care of the dog, the care of the body as a precondition and precursor of taking charge of oneself. I had swum myself at the same athletic club he had joined and so we discussed the pleasure and benefits of swimming.

This real-self activation reached a climax when he made an extremely creative business solution of the problem of his dependence on his Father-Figure boss in the company by negotiating a business deal which allowed him to leave the company with his financial independence secure. At the same time, although he had always previously spent his summer time at his parents' summer home, he began to rent a home for himself and to make plans to build his own summer home.

As he established some continuity in the activation of his real self, he became more and more aware that whenever he activated the real self on his own, whether in a business decision, in exercise, or in recreation, he immediately experienced anxiety and then the numbing, attacking voice which he had to overcome. For example, "Just before I jump in the pool, I have this feeling of anxiety and foreboding and have to fight through it in order to jump in, but when I get in and start swimming it goes away. I think it's because I'm doing something for myself, I'm activating myself. It was the same when I bought my house, when I bought the dog. It's the same when I try to concentrate on myself here with you."

For a third example of treatment of the impaired self in the Borderline Personality Disorder, let us consider the treatment of the young woman, Jean.

Clinical Example: Jean

First year: Three times weekly. My confrontations with Jean were as follows: Why didn't she take better care of herself, her appearance, her apartment, her job? Why did she let other people dump on her? Why didn't she activate and support herself? This issue became clarified in the first six months of treatment around discussions about two boyfriends whom she was then dating. One seemed healthier and more genuinely interested in her, but he made her so anxious that after dates with him she would have to "pig out." Then she would avoid him. The other boy, narcissistic, clearly tried to exploit her solely for sexual purposes. She reported liking him and daydreaming about his caring for her. Her fantasy about the narcissistic boy was as follows: "He wants me. The rest of the world doesn't exist; it's just me and him—perfect. He's there—the first time anyone put me first."

Confrontation of the maladaptive vicissitudes of her defensive self in these two relationships made her aware that when she acted in a mature, independent fashion with the boy who really liked her (*her real self*), she became very anxious, "pigged out," then wanted to avoid him. On the other hand, the one who was exploiting her reinforced her defensive self and relieved her anxiety about being independent, and she therefore felt better with him, although she was allowing herself to be abused, which inevitably ended up in reinforcing her bad feelings about herself. She integrated this confrontation, stopped seeing the narcissistic boy, and tried to maintain a relationship with the healthier one, but without much success. She was not yet ready to activate her real self in an autonomous and independent fashion.

At one point, after a particularly neglectful act on the part of the mother, the patient had an outburst of rage and binging, recognizing for the first time that she was expressing her anger and disappointment at her mother by the overeating. However, this recognition was quite superficial and did not last. She began to suspect that maybe she felt that her parents expected her to "screw up."

In the second six months she gained somewhat better control of her defensive self, affect began to emerge, and her ability to stay in touch with it improved. Work on her feelings and perceptions about herself and on her relationship with her parents moved to center stage. Her real self started to emerge with its associated abandonment depression. She felt cheated, that she had been given nothing: "I'm stuck, and I don't feel I deserve it. I'm a bitter sufferer. My self is not important; I'm wasting my life away, lonely and depressed, so sick of no place to belong, I feel deserted. It's degrading to feel like nothing. I can't enjoy anything because of self-hatred. I'd just like to curl up and die. I feel dead, hopeless and might as well daydream."

This session activated the patient's defensive self. She stayed in bed the next day, didn't go to work or come to the next session. "I didn't care. I felt helpless, alone, nobody loves me. It's unfair. Everybody has their own life, and I'm stuck, and I have no self. I want to feel needed, special, loved."

She now began to investigate the past: "As a child I always felt that way, but I also thought mother was so wonderful. She let my brother sneak into her bed. I tried to sneak in, but they wouldn't let me."

Jean: Second year. By the end of the first year, the patient's perceptions of parental scapegoating were deeper and more continuous. "My emotional instability is related to not being noticed or cared about. My failure is a reflection not of me but them. I felt like a 'thing.' All they seemed to care about is that they failed. How dare I think of failing and being depressed? It's like stabbing them in the back. My mother is so sweet on the surface. She makes me feel so guilty that I want to cry. They just want to be free from the burden of guilt. My father would sacrifice anything for his pride and selfishness. How come my mother was never there for me? How dare she treat me as if I'm nothing? How dare father tell me I should slave for him?" Here, for the first time, the patient is beginning to mobilize her aggression to support herself. The internalization of aggression defense is beginning to yield.

However, after the session she again became overwhelmed by guilt and depression, activated her defensive self and "pigged out," and then detached. It took several sessions of confrontation of the link between affect and defense to get back to the theme. For example, several weeks later she returned with: "Mother is a pitiful working machine; father is a fraud, a fake, callous. I am a lost, helpless soul who belongs nowhere. My parents always have somebody else to blame, mainly me. They haunt me. They got me. I have no self. I'm at the bottom of the barrel. They wanted a boy, felt guilty about me, treated me as if I didn't exist. I had to bear their guilt."

This interview discharged some rage and depression, and the patient's real self again emerged. She said: "I felt good after that interview. When I'm not off in a daze, I mean the detached state, I realize I'm smart enough to do anything, and I felt good about myself. But most of the time I believe I am the daze." I pointed out to her how the actor can become the role. Jean now was beginning to fight off the detachment defense after these sessions filled with rage and depression.

Several months later, the emerging real self, the soundness of the therapeutic alliance, and the establishment of working through were further evidenced by a dramatic change in her appearance: she stopped dyeing her hair red, removed the makeup and spiked heels, and appeared as a natural 18-year-old brunette. She said proudly: "It's me." She also became more interested in singing and began to look for auditions with local bands. She was starting to express her newly restored self in reality. Still the enormous struggle with depression, detachment and daydreaming continued.

A month later she was able to say: "I can see my own life coming together for the first time." About 18 months into treatment, a dramatic incident occurred showing a further consolidation of the real self and self-supportive behavior. The mother again rewarded her regressive behavior and the next morning she felt terribly depressed. "I didn't want to get out of bed, so I didn't. It's a constant battle. Then I felt overwhelmed, helpless, couldn't go on, couldn't handle it. Then I decided the hell with everything. I'm going to do something for me. Let them worry about it." In other words, she transferred affective investment from the object to the self representation.

She took off for two days by herself to think just about herself and let the feelings come. The parents called me in a panic and all I could say was I didn't know where she was but I thought that she was probably in no harm. On her return she said: "I decided I had me, and that's all I needed. I have to take care of me and not be so concerned about them. I have to break the pattern. I had to make a choice for myself and take the consequences, and now I have to follow through. I'm ready to do for me. I feel a solid grasp, a solid perspective."

Nevertheless, she continued to behave in the same compliant role with her parents, although she saw less of them.

Now the theme which had been played out in the environment began to emerge purely from her psyche: Her attempts to activate her real self precipitated all the symptoms which had formerly been precipitated by interactions with her parents. They would activate the defensive self and she would become depressed, binge, feel exhausted, detached: "When it's most important to support myself, it's most difficult. After the last interview, I felt positive about myself, but then I did it again. I gave up and cut off feeling and wanted to 'pig out.' I'm scared to death of that other person who gives up and wipes me out—who pulls the wool over my eyes" (*the defensive self*).

The progression-regression continued through the next several months. The persistence of regressions suggested that she might not be able to maintain the continuity of containment of affect necessary to create the conditions to work through the abandonment depression. I began to doubt her capacities. Did she not have the basic ego strength to work through? Was she part psychopathic or had she been so rewarded for regression that she was unable to give it up? Or was she so masochistic that she could not give up the pleasure of the punishment?

I brought these concerns to her attention by saying that it seemed to me that she floated back and forth on issues about which she was quite clear and that I was uncertain whether she did this because she was unable to control her behavior or because she chose not to. I noted that I did not observe the kind of struggle that would indicate that she was trying but unable to control her behavior. I wondered why she seemed to give up on her self. This led to a renewal of her efforts to activate her real self.

Jean: Third year. Paradoxically, as Jean began the third year of treatment, for the first time she reported managing her separation panic about being alone without her defensive self: regressive acting out, detaching, or overeating.

Several weeks later, in the setting of a separation stress due to my going away for a week, Jean again reported more mastery of her separation panic: "I left here scared. I went back to the apartment and realized that if I didn't instantly force myself into action, the infant would take over and I would give up. I felt desperate, and I went jogging without even changing clothes. Afterward, I felt so relaxed and so good." The commitment to her self representation had overcome the regressive urge. I reinforced her efforts at mastery by saying: "Good for you"—the kind of affirmative, encouraging response for real self activation she had never received.

She continued: "But then, if I keep it up, I feel so lonely and angry at my fate, I have to blow it." These reports allayed for the moment my doubts as to her capacity.

Several weeks later the patient reported a dramatic dream outlining her withdrawing object relations part-unit in the following context: "I was rereading my diary about my relationship with my parents, and I saw it was the same now as it was five years ago, and I just wanted to give up. I couldn't sit there and feel bad, the anxiety, so I binged. I wanted something to knock me out and put me to sleep.

I went to sleep and had the following dream: My mother was there telling me what to wear, but she didn't look like my mother. It was another woman, scary, with wicked eyes, a strange woman, a witch, an ugly monster who resented me, had it in for me. I was desperately trying to put the face of my mother back on the witch, trying to tell this woman with my eyes not to turn into the other woman, not to turn into a witch. I was holding my breath, and finally I was able to see my mother."

Her free associations were: "I'm desperate to continue the fantasy of a loving mother. I can't bear to see anything different." She recalled a memory of how she defended against these feelings. "As a child I always used to feel uncomfortably blank and bored. I felt the same this morning when I had to drag myself out of bed to go to work. I wanted to quit. I was exhausted. I am brainwashed. It's too much to fight; I give up. I even want to get rid of my boyfriend so I can feel sad. Everything I live for and believe is a lie. My heart bleeds for myself and my innocence. Could it have been possible in the family that I was the good person? I have the urge to hurt someone, my boyfriend, to make him feel as I do. He loves me so I can hurt him, as I let them hurt me. I am the ugly person with the sick, demented mind."

I interpreted that she seemed unable to handle the anger, disappointment and depression at the perception of the mother's scapegoating (the withdrawing object relations part-unit), that she would have to face these feelings about the witch in her head which were activated (the withdrawing object relations part-unit), every time she tried to individuate. She would have to master it in her head or it would continue to interfere with her emerging self-activation. She replied that when she sees the anger she panics and takes the anger out on herself by giving up and beating herself up.

The increasing capacity to contain and work through her abandonment depression rather than regress and act out to defend were illustrated in her reaction to my next vacation. She complained in the last interview of feeling empty, bored and depressed and then reported the following dream: "I saw my little cat jump from a balcony, knew it was too high, screamed for help but no one heard. The cat jumped and was smashed on the floor. A helpless, innocent thing? Why did she leave me?" Her free associations: "People put me so low. There is nothing to myself! What difference could I make? I remember feeling this way when Mother had my brother. And then she ignored me even more."

For the first time I interpreted that she was reacting to my impending vacation as if it were a repetition of her mother's un-availability.

DISCUSSION

Origin of Borderline Triad

The parents verbalized love and affection despite their mutual neglect of Jean's individuative needs, and these verbalizations formed the basis for Jean's rewarding-unit fantasy. The father's negative feelings about dependency were projected onto the pa-tient; the mother's negative feelings about independence and her depression were projected onto the patient.

Clinical Picture of Borderline Triad

Jean identified with these projections at the cost of her own individuation. Her self representation of a good, obedient child, linked with the affect of this unit—being taken care of, was allied with a pathological ego which required avoidance and denial of individuation, along with clinging, helpless, childlike behavior. The painful affects of separation panic, homicidal rage and suicidal depression were managed by detachment of affect and binge eat-ing. She presented herself as a helpless, clinging, compliant, "beautiful" child who on the surface was loved for her childlike behavior but who underneath was bad and wrong for her de-pendent needs.

Therapeutic Management of Borderline Triad

This false defensive-self, detached-affect facade had defeated the efforts of therapists to penetrate it for three years of psychotherapy and was the first clinical problem in treatment. In order to minimize regression and maximize the need for responsibility and self-activation, I required that she move out of her home and get a job in order to have to take care of herself. I began the task of dealing with the pathological ego through confrontation of the maladaptive and self-destructive aspects of her avoidance and clinging behavior, as well as on the detachment of affect involved in binge eating. As a consequence of internalization of my confrontations, her real self started to emerge: she began to take better care of herself, activate herself, and try to act in a more mature and independent fashion. In addition, she attempted to get hold of and control the acting out through the detachment and binge eating. A pattern emerged of progressions that would lead to temporary control and movement ahead, followed by overwhelming need for regression. This process occupied the first year without the patient becoming aware either of the underlying affects that the regressions served to deal with or of what precipitated these affects.

In time, as she became better able to activate her real self and to continuously control the false defensive regressive self, she became more and more aware of two types of precipitating factors which produced painful affects which required regressive defense: (1) self-activation or individuation movement itself; and (2) environmental separation experiences including parents' neglect or seduction.

There was also a relationship between the degree to which she was able to activate herself and the type of man she formed a relationship with. During the first stage, when she could not activate her real self, she had a very destructive boyfriend—a repetition of the relationship with the mother: She had fantasies of loving and being loved by him, while in actuality he was narcissistically using her. As she moved into the second stage, her real self began to emerge and she became better able to take care of herself and to activate herself. She dropped this boyfriend and the next one at least verbalized and attempted to treat her more appropriately, but he, himself, was not able to be available because of his own problems.

After the second year of treatment, as her self-activation con-solidated, she was now in her own apartment and managing both that and her job. A third male entered the scene who was the most appropriate so far in his feelings and behavior towards her. The regressions had become fewer and she had become more and more in touch with separation panic, homicidal rage, suicidal depression, and a profound lack of entitlement of self.

The progressive and regressive vacillations have often impelled me to seriously question whether Jean had the capacity to indi-viduate and free herself from the bonds of the abandonment depression and separation panic. This issue, however, could not be put to the fundamental therapeutic test until the later phase of treatment where it was seated securely in her psyche rather than in the environment, i.e., where Jean perceived that any move toward self-activation or growth brought on a separation panic which she responded to by regressive defense. The issue had been joined and progress was maintained, but its final resolution still remains in doubt.

The case illustrates how the therapist uses the therapeutic tech-nique of confrontation of the patient's pathological defenses to eventually bring the patient to the awareness of the operation of the borderline triad within her own psyche: *Individuation* leads to *depression* which leads to *defense*. It is the patient's awareness that this triad is deeply internalized and automatically triggered by precipitating stresses of separation and individuation that secures the therapeutic alliance and binds the patient to treatment as the alternative of choice in dealing with her borderline problem. At the same time the therapist utilizes the therapeutic technique of communicative matching to reinforce the consolidation of the emerging real self.

COMMUNICATIVE MATCHING WITH THE IMPAIRED SELF OF THE NARCISSISTIC PERSONALITY DISORDER

Clinical Example: Harold

As Harold began treatment, he was working for one of his family's companies, living in a luxurious apartment, and relating to his narcissistic but beautiful wife exactly as he had to his mother. He idealized her, was dependent on her, and organized his life around trying to please her except where it conflicted with his need to please his mother. His wife's leaving him precipitated a challenge to his intrapsychic structure and created a first opportunity for the emergence of his real self. Would he respond to this separation stress through totally narcissistic defense, i.e., his grandiose self, or would he attempt to use it as an opportunity to activate his real self to reorganize his life?

The first efforts at communicative matching began when it became necessary for him to settle the financial aspect of the divorce. He was tempted, because of his need to please her, to deny and ignore financial reality and offer her a very unrealistic settlement. Besides confrontation of his denial of the destructiveness of this approach, there was much communicative matching discussion of the realities involved in divorce settlements, such as the need to get a reliable lawyer uninvolved with either wife or family.

With the settlement of the divorce, the next question that arose was whether to continue in the family company which provided him with titles and money but no opportunity for real-self expression. Also, should he stay in the expensive apartment which provided narcissistic supplies but was entirely too big for him in his present situation?

He decided to leave the business and completely separate his own finances from those of his family. This required extensive negotiations with the mother, of whom he was terrified. Beyond the confrontation of his submissive behavior with the mother, we discussed various reality aspects of negotiation where it was important for him to keep his own objectives in the center of his mind. With great struggle and difficulty he was able to make a settlement with both his mother and his wife more on the basis of the real self than his grandiose self. Then he sold his apartment and moved into smaller, more appropriate quarters.

This provided an opportunity as he brought in each clinical example to discuss with him the reality and vicissitudes of real estate in New York City, as well as the problems between real estate agents and people buying apartments. He managed to achieve this move more on the basis of his real self and now was free, at least financially, of wife and parents in his own apartment. These changes altered his environment and lifestyle from one that was regressive and defensive, in the sense of both work and relationships resonating with his grandiose self at cost to his real self, to a more adaptive style where he was now free of these regressive relationships and confronted with the necessity to activate his real self on his own as a guide to manage his life. These changes also, of course, interrupted his defenses and brought to the surface his abandonment depression and his difficulty activating the real self, as described in Chapter III.

Confronted with the need to find something to occupy his time and to choose a career, the difficulties with the real-self activation created an enormous problem. He couldn't decide what he wanted to do. He had trouble concentrating. He was ambivalent about all interests and activities. He was afraid that he would fail, afraid that he would be humiliated and put down in whatever direction he chose to go. He also became intermittently overwhelmed with passivity and avoidance. He found himself unable to do anything.

He tried vocational testing to resolve his ambivalence and inability to identify and to activate his real self. This gave me an opportunity to communicative match by discussing with him the reality that what was most important was not his abilities—which were excellent as indicated by his excellent grades in graduate school—but what he wanted to do and his motivation. The vocational testing would not settle that for him.

The problem was further complicated by the fact that he now had sufficient funds so that he did not have to work to earn money. Again, this provided an opportunity to communicative match by my pointing out that money can often be a handicap and that most people have to work in order to earn a living and therefore have no choice. The luxury of not having to work provided an enormous range of choices which just made his problem of identification of what he wanted to do more difficult. This led to communicative matching discussions of how you go about deciding and the need for experimentation between the real self and the environment in the consolidation of a career or an interest.

Finally, desperate about his inability to decide, he decided to take some classes. "It will force me to go to war or lay down my arms." The courses were in accounting, law and painting. This confronted him with all of his difficulties in self-expression and provided opportunities to discuss in a communicative matching sense the realities involved in these areas of learning. These discussions were aimed at helping him sort out and distinguish between the motivations of the real self and the grandiose self. For example, painting was very attractive to him because of its exhibitionistic aspect, i.e., he would be famous and people would look at him and admire him. This, of course, had to be contrasted with the real self satisfactions of posing oneself a task and mastering or achieving it.

At one point he became interested in investing in a play, did so rather impulsively, and was terribly disappointed when the play failed. I had a communicative matching discussion with him about the realities involved in play investing that one should keep in mind, i.e., a small percentage of all plays succeed and it requires someone with great judgment and experience in the theatre in order to insure success.

Jogging became one of his main activities, which posed a unique problem: On the one hand it was defensive and regressive in that it resonated with the grandiose self; on the other hand, it also was an expression of his real self.

His emotional response to running would vacillate back and forth from grandiose self to real self. For example, historical material on the abandonment depression would emerge in sessions and he would then throw himself into the running. The excitement of the physical activity and the release of endorphins resulted in a kind of manic stimulation of the grandiose self based on his performance. At the same time, the material related to the abandonment depression would disappear from sessions. Yet he did have athletic ability. It was stressed that it was not necessary to run only to deal with his bad feelings about himself but one could run in order to express the real self in taking good care of his body, making sure it was in good shape, and enjoying the physical pleasure of running and competing.

Again and again it was necessary to raise the question of whether his classes in accounting, law, and painting were to be hobbies, recreational pursuits, or his main lines of interest. In connection with the painting, it was necessary to emphasize that if this were to be his main line of interest, he was to be a novice for a long time, competing with experts and professionals in these fields. Therefore, it would be difficult for him to expect much environmental success.

He was investing the money that he possessed on his own and having a substantial amount of success which he regularly devalued since it didn't meet the criteria of his grandiose self. This attitude was confronted but also communicative matching occurred through discussions with him about the difficulties that most people have investing. He seemed to have overcome his anxiety and wondered why he did not use this particular interest as a basis for a career.

His relationships with women after the divorce presented similar problems between the grandiose self and the real self. He expected women to admire him, to devote themselves one hundred percent to him. He would have many one-night stands, would not take women out in the formal sense but expected them to show up when he called. There were no continuing relationships. He expected to be admired and to have his sexual performance applauded.

In this operation of the grandiose self with women he felt confidence, entitled, secure, without anxiety about performance. The inevitable closed circle of endless repetition of these empty encounters began to deprive them of their defensive value and his loneliness, isolation and depression about relationships came more to the fore. He began to reexamine the question and to attempt to activate his real self with women. As a result, his feeling state changed totally to one of inadequacy and certainty of failure and rejection.

The most fundamental ideas of how one realistically goes about establishing a relationship were foreign to him and had to be discussed through communicative matching. For example, he had to learn the difference between the chemistry or sexual attraction and the personality of the other person; how the relationship begins with the former but its endurance is based upon the latter; that one checks out the latter before getting too much involved with the former; that if one expects a realistic relationship, one has to pay as much attention to the other person's self as to the expression of one's own; that as with work or career it is necessary to experiment in order to determine exactly what type of woman best fit his real self.

He had been accustomed to picking only extremely beautiful women because they were an exhibitionistic, narcissistic supply. They made him seem more important to others. To pick a woman because she suited his emotions and his real self was a novel and threatening idea. Along with this, of course, he had to work through the fact that his disappointment in women was mainly due to their not being perfect and not resonating with his grandiose self.

Again, it must be kept in mind that along with this entire process he was working through his abandonment depression with extremely painful affects of depression, rage, hopelessless, and helplessness.

Clinical Example: Walter

Walter was devastated when his wife left him. This was made even worse by the fact that he lived in a suburban house with adolescent children and had to move out of the house. This, of course, also stimulated an environmental opportunity to activate his real self. However, his initial response was one of total apathy and depression, and a kind of sit-down strike. He refused to think about the problem and refused to move; what had been his mainstay in life, his work, also began to deteriorate. He was too depressed to be able to manage this situation. He would feel "embarrassed to admit I'm not managing, angry, I feel stupid, painful, humiliated, and I feel nothing but loss. I'm holding onto the old ways because I'm afraid to begin the new. I'm waiting for magic, am immobilized."

I introduced communicative matching by questioning why activating his real self now to manage was so threatening since most people experience excitement and pleasure at the prospect. He finally got himself to move out impulsively into an apartment which was really poorly suited for him. This led to discussions of the kinds of apartments he might choose which would suit his position and experience in life.

Once in the apartment he collapsed into a funk even to the point of making no plans to see his adolescent sons, with whom he was very involved. This presented an opportunity to discuss the effects on the sons of his distancing himself from them and contrasting them with his wish to be a good parent. His adolescent children were managing the separation better than he and this was used to encourage his activating his real self.

Very slowly and painfully he began to activate his real self, contacted his sons and began to see them, which led to many discussions of differentiating the sons' needs from the father's needs, and the need for the father to father the sons. His interest in his work returned and he began to utilize his real self in sessions to reevaluate his relationship with his wife, not from the point of view of the loss of his entitlements but rather from a realization of the reality that he had provided little emotional satisfaction for her. This provided the opportunity for communicative matching about a husband's role with his wife and what kinds of gratification he provides her, and vice versa.

The turn towards the real self now shifted his perspective about work which had always been egosyntonic. He began to see that his satisfaction at work was a combination of mastery and achievement as well as arising from his being the center of attention and the unique, idealized figure for his entire staff. He began to see, also, how he created antagonisms among his peers with whom he was a consultant because of his arrogant, harsh and devaluing behavior.

This led to discussions of collegiality between peers, of the need to give realistic acknowledgment to other people's self if he expects to have relationships with them, of the satisfaction of the real self at work through mastery and achievement of the tasks imposed by the work. Since work had been the mainstay of his life, it did not pose the same problem as in the case of Harold discussed above. It was necessary only to work with his use of work for narcissistic purposes as opposed to the purposes of his real self; when these were differentiated, it was necessary to point out how work gratified the real self.

However, there was a good deal of communicative matching about work habits. He had been a workaholic in that the work itself reinforced his narcissistic armor and emotional detachment. He began to see that his schedule was "unrealistic" as we had discussions about "the schedule is made for the man, not the man for the schedule." He also began to see the need for time to pursue recreational interests as opposed to work.

Probably the biggest arena for communicative matching was his relationship with women. He had had almost no dating relationships prior to marrying his wife. His whole perspective was dominated by his sense of narcissistic entitlement, his feeling that he should be the center of attention of the woman's life and that, like his mother, she should subordinate herself to him in all ways. In the same way as with the prior patient, it became necessary through communicative matching responses to discuss the realites of how the real self forms a relationship as opposed to the narcissistic self. He found this extremely difficult to do.

Despite this, as a financially secure professional man, he soon became the center of attention for a number of women who actually chased him. He would form instant intimacy relationships based on their providing social and sexual gratification but when they would present their needs for a more enduring relationship, he would explode with narcissistic rage and drop them.

This kind of reaction led to opportunities to differentiate between the narcissistic and real self. He would impulsively initiate sex with women without finding out what their personalities were like, only to recoil in disappointment and rage when he discovered their handicaps, inadequacies or demands for permanent relationships. He had difficulty distinguishing whether he really liked the woman from his liking of her mirroring of him; it was more often the latter. He would say: "I haven't learned how to be friends with women. I may only be attracted to women who see me as king or potentate and who belong to me and let me control them."

Finally, the day came when he said: "My real self is beginning to emerge. Although I'm not clear who I am, I am no longer a potentate or star, but there is more to me than that, there is something coming out that is authentic and real." He began to experience, as he called it, a profound change in his lifestyle as his real self emerged. He was enjoying his mastery at work, relating more to his colleagues on a real basis and getting good feedback, had more recreational time, had lost his restless, impatient, impulsive actions, was able to view himself and others, particularly women, more realistically and to experiment with his real self. "I'm trying to contain and think rather than act. I'm less afraid or uncomfortable with myself, more willing to try to understand what other people's needs are." Initially, however, he found that, as he attempted to experiment with the real self and with women, i.e., relate to them on the basis of a liking for them, when they began to respond, this response would immediately trigger his grandiose self and he would lose interest in their real personality except as a narcissistic supply.

After much experimentation, he found a young, single, attractive woman, about 10 years younger than he. Again he has "instant intimacy" with her, begins to see her exclusively, decides that he's in love with her and her with him, and anticipates marrying her as he is in the terminal phase of clearing up his divorce. She wants a child. He tells her he does not and denies to himself the eventual problems involved with this woman who has never before been married and wants a child.

He had had to change firms because his company was going out of business. In his search, he ended up with a bad "fit" since he did not adequately examine and research the firm that wanted him. He soon found that his co-workers were quite mediocre and the combination of his outstanding ability and his narcissistic manner had them up in arms against him within a few months. Finally, he had to sever the relationship.

There was much communicative matching discussion of the politics of law firms and also of the concept that anyone who attempts to raise his head above his peers has got to anticipate some envy. Again, Shakespeare's "Julius Caesar" served as an example.

It would appear that the effectiveness, or airtightness, of the grandiose self-defense in the narcissistic disorder results in the real self being placed in isolation. As a result, it is not available for experimenting, testing and learning in interaction with the environment. Therefore, as it begins to emerge in treatment, all of these relatively obvious and almost commonsense notions about the reality of life and interactions between people have to be not relearned, but learned for the first time. Although the communicative matching process is the same with the borderline and the narcissistic personality disorder—unlike the technique of confrontation which is used differently with the two—one has to be careful in the latter disorder to know whether or not the communicative matching is being co-opted by the grandiose self and leading to resonation with the grandiose self and further resistance.

Part 2

SOCIOCULTURAL

Clinical work on the repair of the impaired real self inevitably leads to questions as to what social and cultural influences foster or inhibit its development and expression. Although the pursuit of these questions on an anecdotal or experiential level does not have the same validity as clinical evidence, it still provides important food for thought. This section presents some hypotheses and speculations about the relationship of cross-cultural and sociocultural factors to the development and expression of the real self. The aim is to extend and elaborate on the clinical concept of the real self rather than to present sociocultural research for its own sake.

CHAPTER VI

The Development of the Real Self and Maternal Libidinal Acknowledgment: Cross-Cultural Approaches

The preceding chapters described the vital role of maternal libidinal acknowledgment on the development of the real self in the American culture, which places great emphasis upon maintaining maternal libidinal availability for the emerging self. The preservation and enhancement of this intimate early tie between mother and child takes much time and effort.

The question is often asked: "Is all this emphasis on maternal libidinal availability really necessary for the development of the self?" We can offer some evidence on this question by considering other cultures who have handled the matter quite differently. Israel and Japan will serve as the basis for our discussion.

ISRAEL

Bruno Bettelheim treated autistic children at the Orthogenic School in Chicago in a residential treatment center without their

93

parents. He became interested in the kibbutz children in Israel because of the de-emphasis in the kibbutz of the early mother-child tie by the taking of the child away from the mother for placement in a nursery. The Israeli were essentially doing with normal children what he had done with autistic children—raising them away from their parents.

The form of this practice has changed greatly in recent years. Where it is done at all, much greater and more consistent efforts are made to maintain the tie with the mother. Nevertheless, this early experience is useful in providing a contrast to the American style. Bettelheim studied the issue briefly (according to local observers, all too briefly) and reported his results in *Children of the Dream* (1969).

He described two reasons for kibbutz form of child raising: (1) It was a frontier society and the mothers were needed to work in the fields; and (2) the kibbutz workers wanted to get away from the maternal domination that had prevailed in the ghetto.

The children were taken away from their mothers at several weeks of age and placed in a nursery with other children. The parents had no responsibility for daily care but visited in the evening. In the nurseries, the children were discouraged from turning to adults for emotional soothing and relief and encouraged to turn towards each other.

Bettelheim reported that he found no evidence of a symbiotic stage of development, nor of separation anxiety. He argued that the children raised in the kibbutz away from their mothers showed no juvenile delinquency in later development, did not drop out of school, and had no drug problems; they were good citizens, soldiers, and students. Therefore, he concluded that this form of child rearing was superior to that in the United States because of the prevalence in the U.S. of juvenile delinquency, school drop-outs and drug problems. In summary, de-emphasis of the early mother-child tie produces a superior product.

On reading Bettelheim (1969), I noted that despite his conclusion that there was no separation anxiety, he presented much clinical evidence that I would interpret as separation anxiety on the part of these children. In addition, in a kind of afterthought at the back of the book, he noted that although kibbutz-raised children do make excellent soldiers, students and citizens, they do have problems in their capacities for essential functions of the real self: intimacy, autonomy and creativity.

Since intimacy, autonomy and creativity, I believe, are the essence of what makes us human, our form of child raising, which places maximum emphasis on the early mother-child tie and therefore provides a maximum potential for the development of the real self with all its capacities including intimacy, creativity and autonomy, is certainly worth the potential price of juvenile delinquency, school drop-outs and drug problems.

Another way of looking at the same issue would be to consider the hero of Philip Roth's book *Portnoy's Complaint* (1969). If Portnoy had realized that the same mother who had contributed, more or less, to his sexual problem had also helped his real self achieve the capacity to write, he might not have complained so much.

The early mother-child tie—specifically mother's acknowledgment of the emerging self—is essential for the development of that self and its potentials for intimacy, creativity and autonomy. Its de-emphasis will lead to deficiencies in these essential human qualities.

JAPAN

The American occupation of Japan from 1945 to 1952 precipitated an increasing Americanization or westernization of this family-centered, group- and state-oriented society. Since in many cultures adolescence is the most sensitive vehicle of social change, this led to a dramatic increase in emotional problems in Japanese adolescents. For example, patricide emerged as a clinical problem. I discovered this inadvertently when my book *Treatment of the Borderline Adolescent* (1972) was published and widely read in Japan. I learned more about these problems recently when I was invited to Japan for a lecture tour which gave me an opportunity to see firsthand the child-rearing practices in Japan, their effect on personality development, and how Americanization had impinged on that process.

Ruth Benedict (1946) described Japanese child rearing as being highly child centered, with the Japanese mother rewarding and indulging her child's infantile narcissism and self-centeredness up to the age of five or six. At that age the mother reverses course in order to socialize the child and uses the emotion of shame to get him or her to control the external expression of infantile grandiosity and narcissism.

We know from our studies of normal development in our culture that the infant's self is both grandiose and omnipotent in the early infant years and that the world revolves around his or her image of self in the dual mother-child fused self-object representation. In the United States this grandiose self must be defused, deflated and brought into reality or down to earth, so to speak, by phase-appropriate frustration at the hands of the mother. If the American mother does not do this but instead, like the Japanese mother, continues to reward and indulge grandiosity and omnipotence, we see in the adult what we clinically classify as a narcissistic personality disorder.

It seems to me that this is exactly what happens in Japan. In the first place, indulging infantile grandiosity is not the same as acknowledging and supporting the emerging real self and self-activation. Secondly, by the time the mother attempts to control the external expression of the grandiosity by shame, it is too late to change the intrapsychic structure. The child has developed a fixated intrapsychic structure, a self representation which is grandiose, omnipotent and self-centered—what we call a narcissistic personality disorder. On the other hand, unlike in the United States where pathologic narcissism is expressed by exhibitionism—a dramatic display of one's uniqueness and marvelousness for others to admire—in Japan the mother's shaming of this external exhibitionism required the child to control the exhibitionism in order not to feel the painful affect of shame. Shame thus became the key affect of Japanese culture, and expressing one's grandiosity and narcissism in indirect hidden behaviors through others became the keystone of Japanese behavior. In other words, the grandiosity and self-centeredness cannot be directly and openly expressed, but must find expression through the other person or group. In the United States we would call this a "hidden" or "closet" narcissistic personality disorder.

If we examine Japanese psychology of interpersonal relations and social behavior, this hypothesis can explain almost all observable phenomena. For example, the most important Japanese theory of relationships is that of Amae elaborated by Doi (1977). The essence of this theory is that the Japanese individual is not expected (as in the United States) to develop to the point of independence where he manages himself and his own emotions; rather he continues to rely on relationships with others (family, groups, state, etc.) to preserve his intrapsychic equilibrium. In object relations terms, he seeks fusion with others to relieve his own internal distress.

In the theory of Amae, the closet narcissist cannot directly express his grandiosity, but seemingly to the contrary, he behaves in a self-sacrificing way to gratify the other person's self-centeredness, with the assumption that the other person will feel guilty and try to identify and gratify his own self-centered grandiosity. Intrapsychically, a dual fused self-object representation is operating which is a direct extension of the early mother-child unity and is similar to the narcissistic personality disorder.

To view it from an intrapsychic object relations perspective, the social values of the family, the community, the state, the emperor are internalized and emotionally invested through the object part of the fused self-object representation. The principal way the grandiose self receives gratification is through this object representation by ostensibly sacrificing its direct expression to the values of the group. The group then provides the narcissistic satisfaction by idealizing the sacrifice. This applies to the style of interaction between two people as well as between the individual and the family, community, state, etc. The best example of the latter is the kamikaze pilot who gains glory (idealization) by sacrificing the self for the state [i.e., the internal object.]

As one might expect, since the principal method of controlling the expression of the grandiosity is shame, the Japanese view normal Western healthy self-assertiveness as being narcissistic, i.e., grandiose, arrogant, vain, etc. The Westerner is being independently self-expressive, not narcissistic, but the Japanese have no model for independent self-expression which is seen as narcissistic; it triggers fear of the shame that it would bring which causes the Japanese to reject it. The importance of the Japanese experience of shame in later life lies not so much in its contemporary sense but in the view of the contemporary experience as a repetition of the terrible infantile experience which must be avoided.

An example of how this operates in interpersonal relations is the following: if a Westerner and a Japanese were spending an evening drinking in a bar, the Westerner, if he were tired, would assert himself openly and directly and say, "I've had enough for tonight, what do you say we go home?" To the Japanese, this is not acceptable. It would be viewed as narcissistic. If a Japanese felt he was tired and wanted to go home, he would say to his companion, "Are you tired, have you had enough?" He is now conveying to him [the object] that the self is tired and needs attention. He cannot do it directly. The companion is expected to perceive this and respond, "Yes, I'm tired. Let's go home."

One of the dividends for Japanese society of this type of intrapsychic structure is the smooth and effective functioning of groups, whether in school, in companies, or in the armed services. We saw Japanese students from first grade to last year of high school throughout the city, all of them wearing uniforms, marching in groups from one tourist attraction to the next.

The thought occurred to me that it would take very little to transform these students into soldiers except to take away their notebooks and pencils and give them guns, for they were already accustomed to functioning in groups. In addition, their social behavior is extremely orderly. They are prompt, efficient, extremely perceptive, and responsive to others' needs. From this perspective, traveling in Japan can be a delight. As might be expected of those fixated at this developmental level, they function far more on intuitive feeling than on logic and they are motivated more by what is best for a relationship or for a goal in a relationship rather than by what is objectively right or wrong.

This pattern of mother-child interaction, producing a narcissistic personality disorder, has profound consequences in Japan for relationships between men and women as well as for how the Japanese society operates. The observable facts are that marriages in Japan are still for the most part arranged by the families to perpetuate the family and are very little based upon love between the two partners. Once the marriage is established, as the Japanese told me, "American men commute to work, Japanese men commute to home." The Japanese man has little relationship with his wife, who is left to manage the home and the children. The Japanese father has equally little relationship with his children, but spends all his time working. It is a workaholic society. He works from early morning until late in the evening, six and sometimes seven days a week. When he's through working, he does not return home to his wife. He may either visit his mistress if he is able to afford one or seek entertainment in the evening with his male friends. Vacations are a rarity. The Japanese claim they must work so long and hard in order to survive and promote "business."

My own theory is as follows: The mother who rewards infantile grandiosity and narcissism beyond its appropriate period and then attacks it and now makes the child feel shame about the very behavior she had been encouraging is abusing the child's developmental needs. I suspect that the Japanese male child gets to the point where he is never going to permit that frustrating, painful situation to be repeated. He is not going to permit himself to be emotionally involved with and dependent on a woman again. This point of view then becomes generalized to society. The men are not going to have emotional relationships with women because of their fear of being shamed and abused as they had been by their mothers, so they organize a society which perpetuates the need for family and traditional values but without emotional involvement between the parents.

The girl is similarly spared the necessity of facing her own problems with emotional involvement. The men deal with the underlying feelings of depression and loneliness first of all by distracting themselves by work and, secondly, by attempting to find that kind of emotional satisfaction in male social relationships. Incidentally, the major theme of Japanese ballads is lone-liness. The women find their satisfaction by immersing themselves in children and the home.

Doi goes to great lengths to explain how Japanese men can be so close without being homosexual. It seems to me clear why this is so. With their narcissistic fused self-object intrapsychic struc-ture, they can project that object upon a man as well as a woman, but what they are looking for is the gratification of their grandiose self in a fused relationship rather than the satisfaction of sexual needs.

To return to the basic thesis of child-rearing priorities and the development of the self, we see in Japan emphasis placed not on the mother's availability and acknowledgment of the emerging real self as in the United States but on her indulgence and en-couragement of infantile grandiosity, followed by an attack upon it. This produces a personality structure which is similar to what we see in the narcissistic personality disorder.

The inevitable emotional price that is paid is the failure of the capacities of the real self to develop, i.e., in the capacities for intimacy, autonomy and creativity. There is no individual auton-omy in Japan. One is not expected to function on one's own; one functions, intrapsychically, through the object and its symbols —family, community, company, state. Most important, there is little creativity. The Japanese are good learners through the proc-ess of imitation, a fact which they fully acknowledge. They do not innovate or create, but they learn and adapt.

As in Israel, we see in Japan that failure to emphasize maternal libidinal availability for the emerging self results in severe diffi-culties for the individual in the capacities for intimacy, creativity and autonomy. In the case of the Israel kibbutz, the adult func-tions but has trouble in his emotional life, perhaps not unlike a higher-level borderline patient in this country who has had de-ficiencies in maternal libidinal availability. On the other hand, in Japan the adult functions more like a local variant of the narcis-sistic personality disorder, but also has difficulties in emotional relationships. My Japanese friends who have read this view com-ment that it is not a question of a better or worse style of child

rearing but one of difference dictated perhaps by Darwinian consideration, i.e., the islands of Japan are so crowded that survival
requires that the major value be placed on the group, not on the
individual. A similar interpretation could be applied to Israel.

The issue has become quite crucial and complicated in Japan
as a consequence of the extraordinary success and affluence of
the Japanese and the powerful thrust of the American influence.
These changes cut right across the center of Japanese psychology
and its customary ways of dealing with the self's emotional conflict and anxiety.

The social evidence consists of the fact that women would like
to enter the work force. They would also like their husbands to
be husbands and fathers; they would like to have emotional relationships and not have arranged marriages. The Japanese men
do not want to devote themselves 101% to their company; they
want to have more time for themselves. There is a broad, gradual
move towards the emergence of a real independent self in this
social aspect of Japanese society. However, Japanese psychology
and development have no provision for an autonomous real self,
nor for dealing with conflicts by assertion of that real self. Rather,
the individual should be dependent upon the group through his
fused self-object representation.

The emphasis of Western values on autonomous real-self assertion is in direct opposition to Japan's own basic psychology of
interpersonal relations, the pursuit of Amae. When they assert
themselves rather than work through the other, they are frustrating this most basic Japanese style.

I strongly suspect that the narcissistic personality structure in
the Japanese has the same defensive function as it does in the
United States: to defend against infantile rage and depression.
Changes in social behavior do not change intrapsychic structure.
Only changes in child-rearing patterns or treatment can change
intrapsychic structure.

Therefore, the Japanese are attempting to assert an autonomous
self in a culture and in a psychology which has always viewed
this as anathema and which frustrates their traditional psychological mechanism of working through the other person. Since

social change does not change intrapsychic structure, they are attempting to do something which they are as yet not equipped to do. A fused self-object representation cannot operate like a separate, autonomous self. The net result is that their defense against depression and anger (the narcissistic fused self-object representation) is going to be interrupted and they will be exposed to the underlying depression and the anger at the original frustration of their infantile needs. They will then act out their anger under the guise of being independent.

This seems to be what is happening. Parent-child psychopathology in Japan today is the opposite of that in the United States. Here we are concerned about parents abusing children. In Japanese society they are more concerned about adolescents abusing parents. The parents act in a self-sacrificing way, according to the psychology of Amae, expecting their children to feel guilty and to gratify their parents' narcissistic self by complying with their wishes. The children, under westernized influence, do not accept the meaning of the parents' behavior. They do not need to follow Amae but need rather to assert themselves like Westerners. They become angry and assert themselves and attack the parents, and the parents do not defend themselves.

But this attack is not based intrapsychically on motives to be an independent self, i.e., healthy self-assertion, because they do not have the required intrapsychic representation of a real self. By rejecting Amae and not working through the group, they have frustrated their own grandiose self defense against an underlying rage and depression. So what on the surface seems like independent self-assertion is really the acting out of frustrated narcissistic rage.

A prominent concern of Japanese psychiatry is "violence in the home." There are occasional examples of violence in the school—teenagers attacking the principal and teachers, bringing all teaching to a halt without the teachers being willing to defend themselves.

I think the effects of Americanization, particularly on the adolescents, is what brought my work to Japanese attention, but the part that attracted them most was the concept of abandonment depression. The Japanese narcissistic personality structure is itself a defense against abandonment depression so that, without their being aware of it, abandonment depression lies at the core of their personality and they feel a kind of automatic empathic resonance with the notion. If this hypothesis about westernization interrupting their defense is true, it augurs for more social difficulty until and unless the Western influence changes child-rearing methods.

CONCLUSION

The Israeli minimized the mother's availability for the emerging real self, thus producing functional adults who had difficulty with intimacy, creativity and autonomy. Japan stresses the mother's indulgence of the self-centeredness and grandiosity rather than the emerging self, thus resulting in individuals with narcissistic personality disorders who, on a social level, function well through groups but have severe difficulties with intimacy, autonomy and creativity. The American focus or emphasis on the mother's availability for the emerging real self preserves the ultimate capacity for these three crucial human attributes.

CHAPTER VII

Sociocultural Values and
the Real Self

Sociocultural values can either potentiate and reinforce or impair and inhibit real-self expression and fulfillment. Contemporary sociocultural forces do not have as powerful an influence as the parents during the vulnerable developmental years of formation of the self; nevertheless, in later years, they do affect the functioning of the self! The more sociocultural values stress the individual's freedom and rights along with his responsibilities, the more they potentiate real-self expression.

If the individual's responsibilities as well as his rights are not stressed, a narcissistic society would result where the most important value would be, "What's in it for me?" Social interaction would deteriorate and the individual would end up in narcissistic isolation, alienation and apathy. On the other hand, the more that sociocultural values emphasize the group and authoritarianism—as in Japan or the Soviet Union—the greater would be the impairment of real-self expression.

The sociocultural forces would influence those who have an

autonomous, fully developed real self differently than those with a disorder of the self. In the case of the former, the positive forces would reinforce and potentiate self-expression and the negative forces would probably be met by the real self with sustained and often effective resistance. The effects on those with a disordered self would be quite different. The narcissistic disordered self would exploit the values of freedom and independence to gain narcissistic, not real self gratification and would fiercely battle the infringement of the negative forces on the individual's sense of entitlement.

The borderline disordered self would react to the positive forces not with greater real-self expression but with greater anxiety about real self expression. It would react to the negative forces as a reinforcement of its pathological defenses.

FROM AUTHORITARIANISM TO INDIVIDUALISM: REVOLUTION OF THE '60S

The revolution of the '60s provides an example of the effects of sociocultural influences.

Authoritarianism could be defined as that standard which requires the individual to submit to and obey the authority simply because of its authority, not because it is right. Obviously this leaves very little opportunity for the individual real self to become activated and experiment. It was the authoritarian attitude of the British monarchy over taxes—among other forces—which impelled the American Revolution, resulting in a society based on freedom and the independence of the individual. Nevertheless, despite this explicit value of our society, many forms of authoritarianism continued to flourish—in child-rearing patterns, in the schools, in the courts, in business, and in social custom.

It is not often recognized that one of the principal benefits of the activism of the 60s was the change in standards in all these areas—a change from authoritarianism to a greater emphasis on individualism. The brunt of this battle for change was borne by the young. Although there was some violence in the activism of the 60s, it was minimal compared to other social revolutions, especially in the light of the changes achieved.

The change toward individualism provided much greater latitude for the real self to explore and experiment with different styles. In the schools students were able to have greater involvement in planning their own curriculum in addition to not having to learn by rote. In the courts there was increased emphasis on civil rights. In childhood rearing patterns, there was greater emphasis on encouraging the child's experimentation rather than on laying down a set of rules. In our social standards there were dramatic changes in attitudes towards dress, towards social roles as husband and wife, father and mother, and towards sexuality, as well as towards the role of women in society with the emergence of women's lib.

This greater freedom promoted the development and functioning of the real self for those who had a fully developed self. However, it also posed more choices and required greater responsibility. Those individuals with a disorder of the self who did not have the capacity to handle the responsibility probably experienced greater anxiety, which required more defense. For example, an adolescent boy, in order to emancipate himself from his parents—i.e., to fulfill the development of an independent self—might feel the need to put a pack on his back and take a motorcycle trip across the country to test his newfound capacities to operate on his own. This would be conducive to his growth and development. On the other hand, a borderline adolescent might take the exact same action, putting a pack on his back and motorcycling across the country under the guise of trying to develop and fulfill his real self, but doing it really in order to avoid the depression associated with responsibility and further development. Thus, it was a form of defensive avoidance of the anxiety and depression that being independent would precipitate.

During the '60s, many borderline adolescents talked about their "need to find themselves," dropping out of school and exploring drugs as a vehicle toward that objective. These activities were not to find their self because they did not have the capacity to find their self. They were attempting to deal with the depression associated with the increased opportunity, freedom and responsibility that comes with "finding one's self."

Sometimes the pendulum of sociocultural values swings too far, as noted by Christopher Lasch (1978) in *The Culture of Narcissism*. He describes how values bypass individualism to go to pathologic narcissism, resulting in an erosion of realistic, adaptive social standards in favor of exclusive, self-centered gratification.

THE SOCIAL ROLE OF WOMEN

The female liberation movement has literally liberated or freed women to divest their psyche of the historical compulsion to fit the distorted and male-determined Victorian ideal of femininity: to compulsively subordinate the real self and its expression; to submissively play the caretaker role of wife and mother rather than experiment and find channels for the development and fulfillment of their real self—including its creative expression as wife and mother.

These distorted Victorian ideals had been passed down from generation to generation by being implanted in early development through parental differences in child rearing attitudes towards boys and girls—i.e., assertiveness was encouraged in boys and discouraged in girls. These notions were then later reinforced by society's dominant attitudes. Truly a formidable combination of forces to overcome.

Female liberation had the power to overcome these obstacles and provide a climate which has allowed women to explore and experiment with their real self, to find and develop new and different lifestyles and more appropriate social roles. This change has drastically altered the historical, traditional role model balance between the sexes and has opened up the relationships between the sexes for further experimentation also in the development of new or different styles more appropriate to the emotional needs of those involved. It is now entirely possible for a woman to decide not to be a mother without incurring a great deal of social disapproval, something that would have been impossible before female lib. Similarly, it is now possible for a man to say he doesn't want to be a father. Conversely, both men and women are freer to creatively explore the possibilities of new parental roles.

The social channels for the fulfillment of the woman's real self have multiplied: professional schools, business, academia. In all areas, women's opportunity for fulfillment have multiplied. The scapegoating of women has greatly diminished. Young fathers are playing a much greater role as caretakers of their infants while women are playing a more active role as breadwinners. As happened in the swing from authoritarianism to individualism, the pendulum of female lib also swung too far in some cases, to the point of denying the complementary differences in the sexes, both anatomical and psychological. The current emphasis on androgeny could be seen as a way of trying to deal with the need to avoid making a new social definition of the differences between the sexes—i.e., the differences are denied.

The Working Mother

One of the most dramatic examples of changes in sociocultural values as a consequence of female lib and other economic factors has been the profound change in the percentage of women in the work force. As of 1983, 63% of women over 16 worked, comprising 43% of the labor force (*New York Times*, July 31, 1984). This greater opportunity for a career has brought with it a problem—how to reconcile a career with having children. Some women attempt to deal with the problem by idealizing one course and devaluing the other: Career is wonderful and Motherhood is not, or vice versa. This approach fails to come to grips with the essential dilemma of how to manage both in an adaptive manner. The competing and complementary aspects of both courses must be realistically faced in order to devise a solution.

The solution involves a complex set of variables that include the emotional health of the mother, the emotional health of the child, the age of the child when the mother leaves to work, the type of relationship between mother and child, and the adequacy of a substitute to take care of the child's needs.

The clearest clinical evidence we have bearing on the subject is the work of Bowlby (1969) on attachment. Bowlby studied the reactions of children who were separated from their mothers between ages 2 and 3 by institutionalization. He found that if the child was not returned to the mother he or she would become angry and upset, cry, complain; he called this the first stage, or the stage of protest and reunion. If the child still was not returned over time, the child then gave up this protest, became depressed, would not play with the other children, would not eat. He called this the stage of despair. However, if the child still was not returned to the mother, the nursing staff would report the child was better and was now eating, sleeping, playing with the other children. However, when returned to the mother, the child showed no interest in the mother except as a source of gratification. He called this the stage of detachment. Bowlby's work, as well as Mahler's on normal development, reinforce each other in their implication that there is in those early years a direct relationship between maternal availability and the development of the self.

Once the child has separated from the mother and has an internal whole image of self and the maternal object, a profound developmental move has occurred for the development of the self and the creation of a very strong ego structure. It therefore seems worth a great deal of effort for the mother to maintain her availability until this point of development has been reached.

CURRENT SOCIOCULTURAL FORCES UNFAVORABLE TO THE REAL SELF

In our society's current scene the lack of extended families, the high rates of divorce, the uprootedness and lack of geographic stability have all contributed to a lack of stability of object relations in the early years and therefore very unstable sources of internalization for the developing and emerging real self. A stability of place and of relatives outside the core family can often provide a stable structural support to enable a child under stress to survive the stress and adapt.

Of equal importance has been the decline in the influence of religion which, in those who are able to believe and to integrate their belief, forms a very powerful regulating force in the developing child's personality. We are now beginning to see a resurgence of this need for religion in the far right of the political spectrum where people are avidly pursuing religious faith.

The negative social forces have a far greater impact on those with a disorder of the self than on those with a healthy self since the less intrapsychic structure an individual has, the more he turns to seemingly stable factors in the external world for stability to help him contain and adapt.

Some sociocultural phenomena are a magnet for patients with a borderline disorder of the self.

The borderline patient with his impaired real self is unable to manage himself and adapt independently. He requires a stable object or an authority to fill his defect in object relations, as well as an external set of rules of guidance to deal with his defects in ego functioning. Any social phenomenon that will provide these two functions—a stable object and a stable auxiliary ego—will be attractive to borderline patients. This does not mean that all participants in the phenomenon are borderline, but certainly borderline patients are attracted to these phenomena.

An example may be seen in the James Jones phenomenon, or such social phenomena as the Moonies or the Hare Krishna sects. All these sects provide an omnipotent object and authority who also provides a guide for living which fills the two defects in the psychic structure of borderline patients. There are some borderline patients who have so much difficulty operating on their own that they regularly and repetitively commit petty crimes in order to be placed back in a prison where they are taken care of. Bad as prison is it is preferable to having to operate on their own. As we saw in the Jonestown phenomenon, the denial of reality involved in the immersion in the sect is great enough to sacrifice not just the real self but life itself.

The religious sects attempt to program the borderline young person into their group by offering him or her a stable object, an auxiliary ego, and the fantasy of love and affection. The programming nature of this enterprise was illustrated by the deprogramming efforts of Ted Patrick who would kidnap the adolescents who had been converted to a sect and place them in a hotel room with another young person who was an expert on the Bible who then proceeded to deprogram them.

I had a consultation with a couple about their only son who was a member of the Hare Krishna sect. The father came to see me when the son wrote him after being a member for several years that his greatest joy in life was to kiss the toe of the leader of the commune. The father related that the boy had had some trouble in high school, underwent treatment, was then sent out west to college, dropped out, and joined the sect. Following this, the father carried on a dialogue with the commune as to which was better, free enterprise or the commune. The dialogue failed. The father was now upset that he had lost a son. All I could advise was that he should probably stop arguing and debating, keep channels of communication open, and at least be grateful that the son was in a sect which was fairly straightlaced and free of drugs.

A similar phenomenon may be seen in the brainwashing of our prisoners of war in Korea and Viet Nam. It could be called psychotherapy in reverse. The individual is not physically tortured, but is deprived of sleep and food, thus weakening his ego resources. He is then isolated with a single interrogator who alternately interrogates and rewards. Over a long period of time the weakening of ego resources and the isolation will impel a borderline individual to unconsciously internalize the wishes of the interrogator in order to relieve his separation anxiety and depression. In this way he is converted. The dynamic for this operation is called identification with the aggressor.

To illustrate how the identification with the aggressor defense operates, consider the movie *The Deerhunter*. (This is not a brief for the movie, but simply a metaphor to explain the dynamic). The American prisoners must play Russian Roulette for the Vietnamese to bet on the outcome. If they did not play, they were placed in the river to drown, so the choices were to shoot themselves or to drown. They were helpless to do anything about it. However, two of the prisoners turn the guns on their captors and escape. Some months later, one of them is found in a Saigon club where the sport is to play this game of Russian Roulette and he is the star. How could this happen? Why would anyone place himself again in such a life-threatening situation? One method of trying to master the external threat of terror and helplessness is to internalize it. Thereby one identifies with the aggressor and repeats the battle intrapsychically. This is the key to the psycho-dynamic of the borderline disorder of the self which is reinforced by these traumatic sociocultural phenomena.

CONCLUSION

The real self, after it has emerged and consolidated in early development under parental influence, still must contend in later adult life with sociocultural forces which may either reinforce or inhibit it.

Having considered the real self from the point of view of early development, psychopathology, treatment, and the effect of so-ciocultural forces, let us now turn to one of its most important functions—creativity.

Part 3

CREATIVITY AND THE REAL SELF

CHAPTER VIII

Personal and Artistic Creativity

Creativity—to invent, to originate, to perceive old patterns in new relationships, or to rearrange old patterns in new ways—is one of the hallmark functions of the real self. The capacity to be creative, like all other capacities, has a genetic or constitutional endowment component in addition to the developmental; thus, all individuals do not have the same capacity.

Creativity is conventionally thought of in the artistic sense, such as painting or writing a book. However, there is a form of personal creativity that has nothing to do with being artistic. This is the individual who through the function of his emerging real self—usually, but not necessarily, in psychotherapy—makes an original, unique creative rearrangement of his own inner psychological patterns, which then becomes expressed outwardly in a new, original, more adaptive, and harmonious relationship with his outer environmental world. In psychotherapy this type of creativity announces itself initially through a specific act. However, over time, it eventually becomes consolidated as a perspective on inner and outer life which is characterized by spontaneity, flexibility, and originality.

Most people probably are aware of and come to fulfill only a small percentage of their potential for creativity, either personal or artistic. There are many possible reasons for this failure. There are no perfect mothers and no perfect children so that all individuals have scars remaining from the period when their emerging self began to consolidate during the separation/individuation stage of development. This does not mean that they have a disorder of the self, but rather that they have later life difficulties which are reflections of more minor conflicts, a residue from that period of time generally seen in problems with creativity, autonomy and intimacy.

Creativity often, but not always, requires effort and struggle and the willingness to endure anxiety. Some people are just unwilling to make the necessary effort or to endure the unavoidable anxiety; as a result, they forego creative fulfillment. Others may have little creative endowment.

The stories of artists' struggles with their own creativity are legend. Some of these difficulties are related either to a disorder of the self or to scars of normal separation/individuation that impinge on their creativity. One of the most common problems is that of avoidance. The artist is unable to get down to doing his work or to follow it through. This is seen most dramatically in so-called writer's block which may often be due to the need of the artist to defend against the painful affects of anxiety and depression which creative expression can impel. The other side of the coin is the artist who is able to follow through, has a great creative success, and then, unable to now endure the consequent guilt, anxiety and depression, turns to drinking to deal with his painful affects.

THE ARTISTIC CREATION AND DEVELOPMENTAL CONFLICT

The more the artist's theme—be he writer, painter, or sculptor—resonates with or expresses a representative developmental conflict of all people, the more likely it is that his artistic product with be popular and successful if it is also well crafted. The best examples of this are those most popular of fairy tales, *Snow White* (1932) and *Cinderella* (1974). On a narrative level, these are stories of a young girl's conflict with a hostile stepmother; on a deeper psychodynamic level, they describe the girl's difficulty with the development of her real self and the defenses she uses to deal with her hostile feelings towards her depriving mother. The reader feels involvement with this story since it dramatizes his or her own central conflict of closeness with and separation from mother, supplies a proxy vehicle for discharge of these feelings, and provides a fantasy solution. No wonder it has been and remains so popular. The rest of us, having gone through the same developmental scheme, have residues which resonate with the basic theme. To borderline patients, of course, this theme remains a central preoccupation throughout the rest of their lives unless they receive treatment.

Let us now examine the two fairy tales from the point of view of developmental object relations theory and the real self.

SNOW WHITE AND THE SEVEN DWARFS

Dramatis Personae

The mother. The image of the good mother is split from the bad stepmother and preserved in fantasy by the dramatic device of her absence through death; she wanted (i.e., loved) the child very much, but died shortly after her birth. It is the blood mother who loved the child but she is no longer there. The same theme is noted in Cinderella.

The father. The father plays no role at all. Both stories describe he relationship between a girl and her stepmother. For example, in *Snow White* the father is mentioned in one line: "After the year had passed the King married a second time." This reflects exactly the role so many fathers of our borderline patients play—a distant, passive, almost nonexistent role.

The queen. The splitting defense mechanism is reinforced by the image of the bad stepmother—she is no blood relation. No effort is spared to make the Queen the very personification of evil with solely hostile motivations. A perfect projection for the rage at the bad mother, this Queen is *all bad*. For example, the Queen is introduced as follows: "His new wife who is now Queen is very beautiful but haughty and proud and vain. Indeed, her only wish in life is to be the fairest in the land." Her narcissism is further illustrated by her addresses to the mirror on the wall—a perfect metaphor for a narcissistic personality disorder.

The stepmother's narcissism and vanity are dwelt upon. For example, after she hears that Snow White is more beautiful than she, she "became alarmed and turned green and yellow with envy and whenever she saw Snow White after that her heart turned upside down within her—that was how much she hated the innocent child for her beauty. These envious feelings grew like weeds in the heart of the Queen until she had no peace by day or by night." This illustrates not only the Queen's rage, but also the central focus it played in the Queen's own emotional equilibrium. The oral quality of her wishes and rage are indicated when the Queen eats with "great relish what she thinks is Snow White's heart."

The Queen's "badness" is elaborated: "You will not be surprised I am sure when I tell you this wicked creature was skilled in the art of witchcraft." Later her sorcery is referred to as "wicked witchery." The child's belief in the mother's omnipotence leads on the one side to good fairies and on the other to witches.

The degree to which her jealousy and envy rankled is suggested in the following: "After Snow White had taken the poisoned apple and was presumably dead the mirror said to the Queen, 'so now thou art the fairest in the land.' " The author then continued: "Now there was peace at last in the heart of the Queen, that is as much peace that ever could be found in a heart full of envy and hate." This description of the Queen completes the defense mechanism of splitting with the good mother image preserved by having the mother who wanted the child die and the very essence of evil projected upon the bad mother, that is, the Queen.

The portrait of the Queen shows a striking resemblance to borderline patients' experience with and descriptions of their mothers. For Snow White's beauty, substitute the patient's individuality and/or femininity or real self. The envy and rage of the patients' mothers are evoked by their efforts at self-activation.

Snow White. The evil of the Queen is contrasted with the innocence and trust of Snow White. Early in the story she is described as an innocent child. Her innocence and trust are later emphasized when she does not see that the Queen is trying to deceive her. This portrayal of Snow White denies any rage on her part and is the perfect complement to the projection of this rage on the bad mother or Queen.

The dwarfs. The dwarfs also serve as the perfect counterparts to the evil Queen who abandons Snow White. They seem to represent a rewarding unit (RORU) rescue fantasy to defend against the abandonment experience. They are small, jolly, kind, genial, and loving; from their first contact with Snow White, they love her and want to make a home for her. For example, they say to her: "If you will keep everything tidy and homelike, you can stay with us and you should want for nothing in the world." Thus, Snow White has been rescued from abandonment by the dwarfs.

The prince. Snow White sleeps, perhaps through her years of latency, and she awakens to become a woman (princess), not through identification with the mother—this is prevented by the splitting—but at the behest of a man, Prince Charming. Another rescue fantasy—a man will rescue her from the trap with the mother.

The Story

The real mother dies shortly after birth of her child and the new, self-centered, beautiful Queen is angry and envious of Snow

White's beauty (*for beauty, read real self*). The Queen is so disturbed that to restore her own equilibrium (*the reason why many borderline mothers cling to their children*) she abandons Snow White to be killed. Incidentally, several patients have expressed the feeling that the only way they could please their mothers was to kill them*selves*.

However, Snow White is saved, or rescued from abandonment, and finds a home with the Seven Dwarfs who are kind and loving, the exact opposite of the Queen. Still angry and frustrated, the persistent stepmother (just like the persistence of our patients' mothers) makes several additional efforts to kill Snow White—first by strangling—which brings to mind the asthma-like symptoms of some of our patients—and second by poisoning—which brings to mind some of the G.I. symptoms patients develop in abandonment states.

Incidentally, as the splitting starts to resolve in psychotherapy and the bad mother begins to emerge, the patients' dreams frequently contain this very theme—that is, if the patient expresses her angry feelings, the mother will kill her. Each time Snow White is rescued by the dwarfs. The last time, when the dwarfs fail, Snow White sleeps through the years and is awakened by the prince and lives happily ever after. The Queen, however, is condemned to dance out the rest of her life wearing red-hot shoes as punishment for her anger and evil.

Thus we have portrayed the essential conflict with the mother—the fear of abandonment, with defenses of splitting, denial, projection of anger, and rescue fantasies.

CINDERELLA

Dramatis Personae

The mother. In this story again the image of the good mother is preserved through her death. The blood mother, not present, had loved Cinderella.

The father. Cinderella's father, although he gets better treatment (four lines) than Snow White's father (one line), still plays no role in her life. "Once upon a time there was a nobleman of France who took a second wife after the death of his first. He did it for the sake of his little daughter so that she would have a mother. Then he left for a journey that would take him a whole year. He believed that his daughter would be well cared for and happy while he was away."

The loss of the father is glossed over and rationalized. So many of our patients are so embroiled in the intense conflict with the mother that in the beginning of therapy their conscious view of a distant father shows striking similarity to the way the author describes Cinderella. Although their father is never around, it doesn't seem to bother them. Of course the anger at the father is defended against and does come out later in therapy. Occasionally, through splitting and projection defense, the father becomes a target for the *negative* image of the mother, the initial anger is expressed toward him, and he seemingly occupies center stage.

Stepmother. The stepmother's role here parallels that of the Queen in *Snow White.* She was a mean, proud woman who cared only for her own two ugly daughters.

The Sisters. In this story, in contrast to *Snow White,* the envy and jealousy are further split off and conveyed not by the stepmother but by the sisters with the complicity of the mother. "Their mother agreed with the sisters that they had best put Cinderella to work in the kitchen."

The Good Fairy. The Good Fairy is the good mother (RORU fantasy) reincarnated to banish Cinderella's feelings of abandonment by magically fulfilling her wishes.

The prince. Again the man, not the father, rescues her from her state of abandonment.

Cinderella. Great emphasis is placed, as in *Snow White,* on Cinderella's kindness and lack of negative emotion. For example, "Cinderella had nothing at all but her own kind heart." The sisters knew that Cinderella had excellent taste and was too kindhearted to let them leave looking anything but their best. At the end of the story, Cinderella's kindheartedness is emphasized again. "She was too kindhearted to leave her sisters lonely while she had so much joy." Not long after, Cinderella married her sisters to noblemen of the court and all lived happily. Cinderella had no anger. No wonder—it was all projected on the stepmother and sisters.

The Story

Cinderella's mother dies after childbirth; the father remarries a proud, mean woman and Cinderella's abandonment begins. The two sisters "had everything (*love*) and Cinderella had nothing (*was abandoned*)." For example, "The sisters had their own rooms furnished with the finest things money could buy. There were silken sheets and satin covers on the beds and velvet curtains at the windows. Early morning they ate breakfast in bed and they never got up until 11 or 12 o'clock. Each had seven dresses. In their jewel boxes there were so many rings and bracelets and necklaces that it took them hours to decide which one to wear. They even had a bird in a cage to sing to them and a round, plump puppy to play with." Is the author trying to illustrate through material things that the sisters "had emotional supplies and Cinderella had none?" Many patients' families substitute things for love.

Cinderella's abandonment is in stark contrast to the "plushness" of her stepsisters' life situation. "Cinderella slept in the attic with the mice who kept her company but did not keep her warm. She often crept back to the kitchen to sleep the rest of the night by the fire. The fire was warm but toward morning the wind slipped down the chimney and blew cinders all over her. She had no dress to change to. She was always dusty and dirty as an old shoe. Her sisters called her Cindertail or if they were in a good mood Cinderella. All day long she washed dishes and scrubbed floors and swept and dusted and ran errands. She ironed their dresses and sewed lace on their petticoats and turned up the hems of their skirts. If they were hungry she ran to the store for candy. They never gave her a bite of it. When they went on picnics she packed their lunches and brought them a bench to sit on. They never asked her to go along or said they were sorry she had to stay behind."

Cinderella's state of abandonment reaches its height when she sees her sisters going to the party: "Cinderella felt so sad at having to stay home that she could not keep back her tears. She ran to the kitchen, sat down by the fire and cried and cried. So pitifully did Cinderella cry that the mice could not comfort her, the fire burned its hardest to warm her but it could not." Her abandonment depression was now beyond repair and at this point her dilemma is resolved by the creation of a rescue fantasy, the Fairy Godmother who then outfits her to go to the party, wanting her to be home by midnight. Cinderella's having to return at midnight brings to mind the great sense of impermanence that our patients have about anything that is going well. It seems as if they are perched on a razor's edge; although temporarily enjoying themselves, they expect to be plunged back into their feelings of abandonment.

On her second visit, Cinderella gets so "involved" with the Prince that she forgets about the time and suffers the punishment. The story ends with the Prince fulfilling the rescue fantasy.

The fear of abandonment, the defenses of splitting, denial, and projection of anger, and the rescue fantasies are portrayed almost as well as in *Snow White*.

The enormous appeal of these two stories rests on the soundest of psychological foundations: the universal struggle over separation/individuation, over closeness with and separation from the mother.

The vivid physical descriptions of Cinderella's deprived state are echoed in the compositions that borderline adolescent patients wrote for school. An example is presented below.

A PATIENT'S COMPOSITION

Case Example: Rich

Poor Rich, living in his own little stone world. A lonely, unwanted person was he. He spent all of his time in a park near the south side of the city. Rich was always there living inside of his own little world. Rain, snow, sleet, he was there in that small, little park.

To this day he still sits by the gates of the park watching the people day and night, coming and going. He felt the longing to be one of them but he was different. Yes, Rich was different. He had no parents, at least he could not remember any. He could only remember that one day when he became a man, before that his memory fails. All through his life he suffered much due to his handicap. He could not communicate to anyone and was never accepted, but was just looked at and usually that look became a stare, an unbelievable stare.

Nights were the worst of all. During the day he watched people doing what normal people do, singing, dancing, dining, talking and enjoying life. But he couldn't move from that cement binding that held him to his destined place. In the day people were around him and he could pretend he was one of those happy people. But at night his fantasies died. No people were present. The park was dark, desolate, cold and lonely. And did he feel lonely. He felt like crying every night but some unexplainable force held him back. It was as if a force was in him saying, "Don't cry, don't give in to this world."

He many times thought of suicide but it would not work for he was immortal. The immortal, lonely, rejected, unwanted of the world. He stood for those unfortunate souls who existed on that wretched planet called earth. He stood for those immortal souls who have always existed and always will.

That forlorn face, that immovable solitude, those torn, ragged clothes. Yes, he was an outcast, and could not cry out for his lips felt like cement, too heavy to move. But one day he did cry out although nobody heard him. And he said to this world, "I hate it, I hate it, I hate being a statue."

ARTISTIC CREATIVITY AND THE REAL SELF

The fully developed real self has access to its creativity. However, the presence of artistic creativity is not necessarily evidence of full development of the self. Many an artist with a severe disorder of the self, but fortunate enough to have talent, draws upon his creativity to find and establish a segment of a real self that enables him to have a higher-level adaptation.

The real self, established and reinforced by his creativity, provides the artist with a harmonious, ego-syntonic system of regulation of self-esteem through self-activation in his art. A fragile and one-dimensional system, it nevertheless rescues the artist from the more usual tragedies of his disorder. Thus, creativity becomes the vehicle of a quest to establish a real self.

Creativity in the quest for a real self will be considered here briefly for the philosopher and writer Jean Paul Sartre and the painter Edvard Munch, and in more detail for the novelist Thomas Wolfe in ensuing chapters.

Jean Paul Sartre

Sartre's own perceptive and insightful account (1964) of his childhood years vividly describes how his grandparents' and his mother's inability to acknowledge his emerging real self and their need to inappropriately idealize him led to a severely impaired real self that was defended against by the false defensive self of a Narcissistic Personality Disorder.

> I was a fake child . . . I could feel my acts changing into gestures. Play-acting robbed me of the world and of human beings. (p. 53)
> I had no scene "of my own" . . . I was giving the grown-ups their cues . . . my own reason for being slipped away; I would suddenly discover that I did not really count, and I felt ashamed of my unwanted presence in that well-ordered world. (p. 54)
> My truth, my character, and my name were in the hands of adults. I had learned to see myself through their eyes . . . When they were not present, they left their gaze behind, and it mingled with the light. I would run and jump across that gaze, which preserved my nature as a model grandson . . . a transparent certainty spoiled everything: I was an imposter . . . The clear sunny semblances that constituted my role were exposed by a lack of being (or of a real self) which I could neither quite understand, nor cease to feel. (p. 52)
> I *was not* substantial or permanent . . . I *was not* necessary . . . I had no soul. (p. 55)

I had neither inertia . . . depth nor . . . impenetrability. I *was nothing*: an ineffaceable transparency. (p. 57)

Sartre's ability to so clearly recall his childhood (an outstanding exception to the rule for most Narcissistic Personality Disorders, who require much work in psychotherapy on their resistance before they are able to revive and remember their childhood traumas) has provided a rich mine for the prospective theorist. Atwood (1963), for example, mining this treasure, emphasized that Sartre's experience of his self and his relations with others as being superfluous, inauthentic and transparent—he lacked a substantial self or identity—was the core psychological theme of his development and that his solution of it was later reflected in his philosophy of being and nothingness.

The developmental, object relations point of view suggests that Sartre's real self was trapped in his Narcissistic Personality Disorder. His fused grandiose self-omnipotent object false self defended against the fears of engulfment and feelings of emptiness, fragmentation and nothingness of his impaired real self by identifying with the idealizing projections of his mother and grandparents. He then performed as a mirroring object to fit their needs. By complying with their narcissistic projections upon him, he became the perfect mirroring object to complete their selves at great cost to his own.

This defensive fusion with the omnipotent object carried with it inevitable fears of engulfment and loss of self. The situation was further complicated by the fact that Sartre's more fundamental fear was that if he did not defend, but instead activated, his impaired real self, he would reexperience the engulfment he had originally felt at the hands of mother and grandparents. His real self was trapped. He experienced it as empty, nebulous, without substance and fearful of engulfment.

Sartre dealt with this dilemma by beginning to write. When his writing was ignored by the family, this loss of mirroring objects gave him some privacy and space to experiment with his emerging real self. He had embarked on a quest that would begin to differentiate his real self from his false self (Sartre, 1964).

My plots grew complicated. I introduced the most varied episodes. I indiscriminately poured everything I read, good or bad, into these catchalls. The stories suffered as a result. Nevertheless, I gained thereby, for I had to join things up, which meant *inventing*, and I consequently did less plagiarizing. (p. 90)

I was beginning to find myself. I was almost nothing, at most an activity (i.e., writing) without content, but that was all I needed. I was escaping from play-acting. I was not yet working, but I had already stopped playing. The liar was finding the truth in the elaboration of his lies. I was born of writing. Before that, there was only a play of mirrors. With my first novel I knew that a child had got into that hall of mirrors.

I split myself in two . . . As author, the hero was still myself; I projected my epic dreams upon him. All the same, there were two of us: He did not have my name, and I referred to him only in the third person. Instead of endowing him with my gestures, I fashioned for him, by means of words, a body that I made an effort to see. This sudden "distancing" might have frightened me; it charmed me. I was delighted to be him without his quite being me. (p. 91)

However, to deal with the fears of engulfment that this quest precipitated, he maintained the split between his false and real self and employed additional defenses against affect such as detachment, distancing and intellectualization; he became an intellectual and a philosopher.

Sartre's Philosophy

The themes of Sartre's dramatic struggle to establish a real self—the emptiness of his impaired real self, his lonely individual struggle to use his creativity to establish a modicum of a real self and his fear of engulfment—all reappear in his philosophy of consciousness, being and nothingness and the human condition (1966). *Being* in itself, i.e., consciousness, is nothingness and non-being has no identity. This idea reflects his feeling of emptiness associated with his impaired real self. Sartre's idea of the radical freedom of consciousness means an acknowledgment that one is the absolute creator of oneself and one's destiny. *Being* for itself. The extraordinary responsibility implied by this role is felt as anguish and a longing arises in consciousness to escape from freedom into the secure solidity of self-identity possessed by things in the world of Being in itself. An individual can escape this freedom only in death.

Sartre as a child had no acknowledging assistance from grand-father and mother for his emerging self and, therefore, had to create it by himself. As a result, he saw all mankind as having to develop a real self without help. The void that encircled Sartre consisted of the emptiness of his impaired real self and the fears of engulfment associated with efforts both to activate that real self and to defend against it with the grandiose self.

Sartre could not see that the emergence and consolidation of a real self could be helped by an acknowledging environment and could be filled with pleasure and excitement as well as struggle. He was equally unable to conceive of an autonomous real self as being complete and whole without fears of engulfment, empti-ness, loneliness or anguish.

His perception of social relationships was similarly distorted by his projections from his childhood, as was his perception of the autonomous real self. He was unable to perceive social relation-ships as emotional sharing and mutual enrichment. In his concept of Being-for-others, he saw relationships as a threat to the auton-omous, contained life of Being-for-itself.

Conclusion

Sartre's quest for a real self led him to writing, which enabled him to activate the creative aspect of his real self while defending against his fear of engulfment and loss of self by splitting, de-tachment of affect, distancing and intellectualizations. His phi-losophy thus became a rationalization of his emotional dilemma of self—being and nothingness.

Edvard Munch

Sartre, through his philosophy, became the rationalizer of the painful affects of the abandonment depression. Thomas Wolfe as will be described in Chapters IX and X, portrayed these affects vividly in words in his novels. Edvard Munch in his creative quest for a real self came to portray in painting, as vividly as Wolfe did in words, the intense affect of the abandonment depression associated with the impaired real self.

Edvard Munch was born in Norway the second of five children. His sister was one year older. His father, an Army physician, was twice the age of his mother, who was already ill with tuberculosis, from which she would die when Munch was five. The mother's sister joined the household to care for the children. Edvard was often sick as a child. He became very close to his older sister who died of tuberculosis when he was fifteen.

These early developmental events placed an indelible stamp on his character that was revealed in his personality and in his painting. He led a nomadic life revolving almost totally around his painting. So great was his fear that he was unable to commit himself to a relationship. His relationships with women were tenuous, sporadic and episodic except for a more prolonged relationship with Mathilde Larsen. But when Mathilde proposed marriage, he literally bolted and ran. He rationalized that women might stand in the way of realizing his true potential for artistic self-expression. His artistic quest for a real self was so tenuous, he could not expose it to the threat of a relationship. He said: "I have never loved. I have experienced the passion that can move mountains and transform people—the passion that tears at the heart and drinks one's blood—but there has never been anyone to whom I could say: 'woman, it is you I love—you are my all' " (Stang, 1977, p. 174). Depression, loneliness and alcoholism plagued him, and he made frequent trips to health resorts, with only modest success. At age 45, his alcoholism worsened, he developed delusions of persecution and hallucinations, and was hospitalized for eight months: "My condition was verging on madness."

His paintings contain the most graphic pictorializations of separation panic, abandonment depression, death and grief. For example, his famous painting "The Scream" is a dramatic evocation of the helplessness of separation panic. He repeats over and over the feelings of loss and abandonment by death in "By the Death-bed" (fever) (1893). "Death in the Sickroom" (1893/94), "The Sick Child" (1885/86), "Melancholy" (1891), "Death at the Helm" (1893), "The Dead Mother" (1893), "Dead Mother and Child" (1897/99).

His difficulties in his perceptions of women were portrayed in his paintings of "Madonna" (1895) and "Vampire" (1893/94), "Separation" (1894), "Separation" (1896), "The Woman (Sphinx)" (1893/94), "Jealousy" (1895).

In the course of a long life (he lived to 81), he produced a prodigious amount of drawings and paintings (over 50,000)—a visual tribute to the extraordinary drive of his creativity and its search for a real self.

The next chapter will pursue the issue of the creativity of the real self further with a detailed presentation of how Thomas Wolfe's creativity came to his aid in his quest for a real self, and enabled him to create a world that vividly dramatized the universal human aspiration and struggle for separation/individuation and the all too common abandonment depression that ensues if this struggle is not supported.

CHAPTER IX

Thomas Wolfe's Quest for a
Real Self—The Struggle

Thomas Wolfe's real self was as imprisoned by his defensive false self as his native town Asheville, North Carolina, was encircled by mountains.

His writing, through a unique combination of individual talent and acknowledgment of that talent by specific and important people in his environment, was the principal vehicle that freed the creative capacity of his real self from that prison just as, in one of his favorite metaphors, the train was the only "way out or escape to freedom from the encircling mountains of Asheville" (Wolfe, 1929).

> The thunder of the great flanged wheels, the long retreating whistle wail had him dream and hunger for the proud unknown north with that wild ecstacy, that intolerable and wordless joy of longing and desire which only a southerner can feel. (Nowell, 1960, p. 33)

The prophetic fantasy of escape of his real self from his psychic prison was to come true, but only for the creative aspect of his real self. The rest of the capacities of his real self remained caught in the developmental arrest, producing a psychological landscape of a towering skyscraper of capacity for creativity standing alone in a desert of impaired capacities of the real self in almost every other sense. He had little capacity for genuine intimacy and little autonomy, he was impulsive and disorganized with little capacity to take charge of himself and guide the conduct of his life.

The activation of his creativity through his writing provided him with a real self whose self-esteem was regularly reinforced by positive feedback from the environment leading to a more or less stable system which also gave him an identity and a style for relating to people. More importantly, from the intrapsychic point of view, the creativity and its expression in writing provided him with an adaptive sublimated defense against his abandonment depression without which he no doubt would have had a far more self-destructive existence.

He suffered from a borderline personality disorder and the development of his real self was impaired by his developmental arrest. His intrapsychic structure—like all borderline patients —consisted of a rewarding and withdrawing object relations part units and a pathological ego and reality ego. There was a defensive self-image based on the alliance between his rewarding unit and his pathological ego in which he avoided self-activation or expression in order to comply with the commands of the rewarding unit to receive maternal supplies.

A unique aspect of his intrapsychic structure was the degree to which he projected and acted out on a grand scale in the environment. He externalized the intrapsychic structures so that the emotional issues were then played out in an almost geographic sense on a broad scale, making them more dramatic and easier to identify.

This intense projection and acting out of his inner emotional states on other people as well as on "the land" emptied out his intrapsychic contents, compounding his states of extreme emptiness which produced a great compulsion "to take in" in order to fill up the emptiness. From a young age he was obsessed with reading, knowing, recording, taking in environmental stimuli:

My brutal and unending efforts to record upon my memory each brick and paving stone of every street that I had ever walked upon, each face of every thronging crowd in every city, every country with which my spirit had contested its savage and uneven struggles for supremacy. (Nowell, 1960, p. 220)

And when he came to write, all of this perceptual material he had taken in returned to him: "Each stone, each street, each town, yes even every book in the library whose loaded shelves I have tried vainly to devour in college returned upon the wings of these mighty sad and somehow quietly demented dreams" (Wolfe, 1936).

THE QUEST

The borderline dilemma was writ large on the canvas of Wolfe's life because of the externalization. He remained caught in the web of unresolved symbiotic dependency upon his mother, motivated by a defensive self which required compliance with her wishes to relieve the severe abandonment depression associated with any moves towards activation of his real self or separation/individuation. This defensive false self was driven by a powerful wish for reunion or fusion with an idealized maternal object in order to relieve the abandonment depression associated with separation and self-activation. However, this wish for reunion and its clinging defense carried with it a companion fear of being engulfed by that object with whom he wished to merge and thereby lose himself.

When his clinging behavior intensified to the point that it triggered too much fear of loss of self—i.e., when he got too close—he would then be compelled to distance himself from the object in order to preserve his fragmentary sense of self. This behavior is often referred to by his biographers as a compulsion to freedom. The issue was not freedom but preservation of self.

The need to distance himself from the object in order to preserve his sense of self brought additional problems. It interrupted his major clinging defense against his abandonment depression, the depression emerged, and other defenses were now required, such as placing himself in a geographic position where he was literally alone and then, to relieve the depression, turning to various forms of acting out such as drinking, sexual promiscuity, and endless, restless, physical wandering.

These themes of reunion and merger, fear of loss of self, distancing, depression, and self-destructive behavior dominated his life and the expression of his feelings in his work. These polar opposites of clinging to the object and then distancing himself and acting out were his principal repertoire of defense until he got in touch with the creativity of his real self in his writing, which then provided an additional, far more adaptive defense.

Thomas Wolfe, like most people, was unable to face the infantile nature of his idealizing, clinging and distancing behavior. Through his enormous creative talent he transformed the issue and expressed it as follows: "It was mostly of a search for a father. Young men sometimes believe in the existence of heroic figures, stronger and wiser than themselves, to whom they can turn for an answer to all their vexation and grief. Later they must discover that such answers have to come out of their own hearts but the powerful desire to believe in such figures persists" (Nowell, 1960, p. 157).

He repeats the theme with Perkins: "You are for me such a figure. You are one of the rocks to which my life is anchored" (p. 157).

In his writing he idealizes the theme in the following way. Speaking of his second book, *Of Time and the River*, he says: "It has to do with what seemed to me two of the profoundest impulses in man. Wordsworth, in one of his poems, 'To a Skylark,' I think, calls it heaven and home and I called it in the first line of my book, 'Of wandering forever and earth again.' By the earth again I mean simply the everlasting earth, a home, a place for the heart to come to and earthly mortal love, the love of a woman, who seems to me belongs to the earth and is a force opposed to that other great force that makes men wander, that makes them search, that makes them lonely and that makes them both hate and love their loneliness. These elements seem to me to be fundamental in people" (Nowell, 1960, p. 172). Wolfe elaborates the theme again through one of his favorite metaphors, the train: "The great train is rushing across the everlasting and silent earth."

Here are the two ideas of wandering and eternal repose. The love theme—the male and female love—also represents this.

Wolfe's clinging to the object was fueled by his idealizing important people in his life: his mother, Mrs. Roberts, Max Perkins, Aline Bernstein. However, as time brought out their realistic inadequacies and his own fear of engulfment and loss of self, his too exacting scrutiny led to disillusionment. These people could not measure up to his need for an omnipotent, perfect object. His desire to escape to relieve his fear of loss of self became so agonizing that it turned his feelings for them almost into hatred. "I see every wart and sore upon them, I mean meanness, pettiness and triviality and I hate these mutations in them ten times more cruelly and bitterly than if I saw them in people that I did not know or cared nothing for" (Nowell, 1960).

This idealization has led students of Wolfe to suggest that his search was an attempt to find not merely a parental substitute but also God the Father of a religion which he intellectually could not accept but for which he still yearned. He turned father substitutes into gods and when he found that they were only fallible and human after all he felt a bitter disillusionment and a sense of having been betrayed (Nowell, 1960, p. 27). Was he searching for a father or to find a religion? My answer to both is no.

During the separation/individuation phase of development, the child perceives the mother as omnipotent and omniscient and craves her acknowledgment of the emerging self (as I have indicated early in this volume) in order that it may separate from the maternal object, become autonomous and whole, and take on its capacities.

It was this that Thomas Wolfe was seeking—a quest for his real self—through the acknowledgment of an omnipotent maternal figure. He had not received this from his mother who used him principally as an object for her satisfaction and, therefore, his borderline fixation left his real self trapped in the developmental arrest. His wish was to be freed from this trap by an omnipotent figure who would acknowledge his real self.

His being trapped in this conflict heightened his perception of this transitional phase between childhood and adulthood, and

sharpened his perception of all of the feelings and images of loss
that any borderline patient with an abandonment depression experiences in psychotherapy as they activate themselves and individuate. His work is replete with extraordinarily poignant,
elegiac, and meaningful images of loss. These images resemble
the poems that borderline adolescent patients write to describe
their abandonment depression (see Rich, p. 123).

This suggests one key to the popularity of Wolfe's books. He
beautifully and eloquently described the vicissitudes of one of the
most important phases of human development. He was the chron-
icler of human aspirations for individuation and a real self as well
as of the extraordinary power and depth of the feelings of loss
involved (the abandonment depression) when the real self's
emergence is not acknowledged by the maternal object. In addition, Wolfe's audience could also respond to his metaphors on
two more mature levels: (1) the oedipal level of conflict, the wish
for the mother as a sexual object versus the wish to emancipate;
and (2) in real later life, the conflict between experiment and
adventure and safety and familiarity.

His life story is replete with the repetitive, stereotyped drama
of his quest for a real self through establishing exclusive symbiotic
dependent relationships with an idealized person, hoping they
would provide the acknowledgment that would free his real self
from its developmental trap. When the intensity of his wish for
merger and fusion became too great, it would trigger his fear of
being engulfed and losing himself in that very merger. He would
then experience enormous fear and have to distance himself in
order to deal with the fear, at which point he would abruptly start
to attack the idealized merger object. The attack was necessary
to enable him to separate and preserve his sense of self. However,
he was unaware of and unable to take responsibility for the conflict, so that he would project, rationalize and blame the idealized
object for all its deficiencies so he could now free himself. But this
left him alone, a wanderer, having to find other defenses against
his abandonment depression.

The unique combination of his writing talent and its acknowledgment from important symbiotic figures in his environment

enabled the creative capacity of his real self to emerge to produce on the level of *adaptation* a unique, artistic product for society, and on the level of *defense* a sublimated, more adaptive defense against and expression of his abandonment depression.

THE LIFE*

The study of Thomas Wolfe's life, through the lens of developmental object relations theory, falls naturally into phases based on his relationship with important people in his life and their relationship to his creativity: first, the long period with his mother through the early developmental years, high school and college, Harvard and New York; then the Aline Bernstein period, the Perkins period, and the post-Perkins period. It may seem paradoxical to categorize a writer's life in terms of his object relations rather in terms of the self, but it is one of the unique characteristics of Thomas Wolfe that these object relations were so essential to the identification and emergence of his real self's capacity for creativity.

Early Developmental Years

Tom was the last of eight children, six years younger than the next youngest, born to a couple who had formed a classic misalliance. They seemed to have come together mostly through a fantasy of escape from their individual fates. The fantasy soon fell apart. Mother was self-centered, domineering, possessive, stingy and greedy, ready to sacrifice any of her children's best interests to her own greed. Father, although sensitive, earthy and lusty, was unable to take responsibility for himself or his family. He was plagued with severe depression which led to catastrophic bouts of alcoholism. He vented his rage at life for requiring him to be responsible by relentless and bitter verbal assaults on his wife and children, blaming them for his dismal life and instilling guilt in his children to motivate them to rescue him.

---

*Much of this material on Wolfe's life is drawn from Nowell (1960) and Turnbull (1968).

Tom, treated as a baby by the entire family, was the object of exaggerated possessiveness by his mother for her last child. She wrote,

> He being the baby, I kept him a baby. He slept with me until he was a great big boy. He wasn't weaned until he was 3½ years old. He still nursed but it was a habit with him, that was all. He didn't really need it. He had beautiful curls, beautiful brown hair. I kept it curled every day. It struck him about his shoulders. He often said they called him a girl because he had curls and wanted his hair cut and I said "Oh no, I want to keep it long you know." So I kept putting him off until it had to be cut but the sad part to me was my baby was gone. He was getting away from me. (Nowell, 1960, p. 23)

He slept in the same room with Mother until he was 12.

It was this profound symbiotic dependent relationship with the mother which on the one hand probably laid the seeds for his rich creativity and on the other hand formed the prison walls of his real self in the developmental arrest. This literal, almost slavish dependence on the mother lasted until the age of 25 when he met Aline Bernstein.

The relationship with the father, though described as happier, seems very much less intense and the father, although having many positive qualities such as his interest in poetry, seems too depressed and involved in his own struggles to be much of a father to Tom. Tom is described as having worshipped him and enjoying literature and poetry with him. The oldest sister Mabel was the father's favorite and the brother Grover (one of twins) the mother's favorite, whereas Tom was her possession.

I am hypothesizing from long clinical experience that the mother's extreme self-centeredness and possessiveness required a compliance on Tom's part leading to the developmental fixation: the development of a false compliant self and the impairment of his real self because the mother would be unable to support the emerging real self which would conflict with her possessiveness. Certainly, nursing to age 3½ and his sleeping in the same bed with his mother suggest her powerful overindulgence of his dependent symbiotic needs to meet her own needs.

Mrs. Wolfe left the father for the first time when Tom was four and took him to a boardinghouse in St. Louis. She left the oldest daughter Mabel to keep house for the father. Tom's brother Grover caught typhoid and died. Tom described his death as giving his mother "the most terrible wound of her life," suggesting that Grover was her favorite. The importance of Grover to her is reinforced by the fact that 34 years later, when she was told that Tom himself was going to die, she reverted to the death of Grover and described it almost word for word as Tom had recorded it in his story (Nowell, 1960).

This reinforces the notion that Grover was her favorite whereas Tom was her possession. In other words, Tom's function was to relieve her anxiety and depression. We could hypothesize that Tom, already overinvolved in a scapegoating, depriving, symbiotic, dependent relationship with his mother, would experience his first external separation stress and abandonment depression in response to her depression at the death of his brother Grover when Tom was four. At this time Tom moved closer to the other twin Ben and would later suffer another loss when Ben would die.

A profound and crucial separation stress initiated Tom's second experience of abandonment depression at age six when his mother decided to leave the father and bought another house to set up a boardinghouse, leaving the father in the original house with the daughter Mabel to keep house for him. The other children "floated in limbo," living at one house or another, but Tom—the mother's possession—had to live with the mother.

Tom wrote in *Look Homeward Angel* (1929): "It was the last tie that bound her to all the weary life of breast and cradle. He still slept with her at night. He was riven into her flesh; forgetful of him during the day's press, she summoned him at night over the telephone demanding his return." There was a bitter struggle between the mother, who demanded that he live with her, and his sister Eliza who supported his wish to continue to live at their father's home where he tried to spend as much time as possible. He hated "the great chilled tomb" of the boardinghouse—The Old Kentucky Home it was called—he was ashamed of it and of his mother's career as a boarding house keeper.

Tom later reported: "I was without a home—a vagabond since I was 7 with two roofs and no home. I moved inward on that house of death and tumult from room to little room as the boarders came with their dollar a day and their constant rocking on the porch. My overloaded heart was strangling without speech, without articulation in my own secretions" (Nowell, 1960, p. 27).

This second crucial separation stress which demonstrates so dramatically the mother's disregard of his best interest—i.e., that of his real self—and her use of him as a possession greatly reinforced his abandonment depression. This required an escalation of defense and set him upon the course that was later to so dramatically influence his life and his work. The omnipotent idealized maternal object with whom he was merged in fantasy had again and again betrayed him and exposed him to abandonment depression with all of its sense of loss and loneliness: first, in the basic nature of the relationship where her self-centeredness, possessiveness, and greed made her unable to acknowledge Tom's emerging self, and later by the depression at Grover's death when Tom was four and the move with Mother at age six. To his prior fears of engulfment and loss of self based on the intensity of the symbiotic union were now added fears of abandonment. The groundwork was laid for retreat into fantasy and the development of distancing defenses. He wrote of himself as feeling "weighted down with loneliness and terror" and feeling he had lost forever the tumultuous, unhappy, warm center of his home (Nowell, 1960, p. 27).

To deal with the feelings of disillusionment, betrayal and loss in this primal relationship, he began to seek defense in self-dramatization in fantasy and in a lifelong search for an omnipotent maternal object which would acknowledge his emerging self and thereby permit him to free his real self from its prison—in other words, he could identify with the acknowledgment of his real self and internalize its strength and wisdom in order to become independent. Fate, however, would compel him to repeat the same disillusionment over and over in his personal life as well as portray it in his writings.

In *Look Homeward Angel* (1929) he said: "The cruel volcano of the boy's mind, the little brier moss of his idolatry, wavered into their strange marriage and was consumed. One by one the merciless years reaped down gods and captains. What had lived up to hope? What had withstood the scourge of growth in memory? Why had the goal become so dim? All his life it seemed his blazing loyalties began with men and ended with images. The life he leaned on melted below his weight and looking down he saw a statue."

In *Of Time and the River* (1935), Tom again idealized and romanticized the search as a search for father. "The deepest search in life it seemed to me, the thing that one way or another was central to all living was man's search to find a father, not merely the father of his flesh, not merely the lost father of his youth, but the image of a strength and wisdom external to his need and superior to his hunger to which the belief and power of his own life could be united" (Nowell, 1960, p. 27).

It was not until he was 37 that he began to see that this quest was hopeless when he wrote: "We never perhaps give up the wonderful image of our youth that we will find someone external to our life and superior to our need who knows the answer. It does not happen—it's not my strength in me but it comes I think from the deepest need in life that all religiousness is in it" (Nowell, 1960, p. 23).

After his painful experience at age six, Tom's behavior took a decisive turn towards fantasy and reading to fill his emptiness. He would spend hours at the library reading every book, good or bad. The use of fantasy and words to defend began to crystallize.

It has been said that our parents give us our problems but also provide opportunities for solutions to our problems. The idealized mother who had betrayed and abandoned him now developed severe attacks of rheumatism and went away for her health every winter, always taking Tom with her, enrolling him in a school wherever they happened to be. The incredible disruption of these travels on the development of peer contacts and latency skills can hardly be overestimated. No wonder that in his later life he had severe difficulties in both areas.

It also indicates how his mother used him as an object. Since she had to go away, he had to go also, regardless of his best interests, just as he had had to stay at the boarding home with her or wear curls and sleep in the same bed with her. The needs of his real self were neglected.

Between the ages of 7 and 13 he spent winters at 8 different places in the south. As disruptive as this was in one sense, in another it introduced him to the idea of using travel as a distancing device to manage his depression and fear of engulfment. It later became an essential part of his lifestyle. In *Look Homeward Angel* (1929) Tom wrote: "Thus did he see first the hillbound, the skygirt, of whom the mountains were his masters. He saw the fabulous south, the picture of flashing field, of wood and hill which stayed in his heart forever. He dreamed of the quiet roads, the moonlit woodlands and he felt that some day he would come to them on foot and find them there unchanged in all the wonder of recognition" (Nowell, 1960, p. 33).

It is possible that after he felt disillusioned and betrayed by his mother at age six when she renewed the pressure for symbiotic merger by these trips, his now reinforced abandonment depression would not permit him to activate the previous reunion fantasy in the same way. Instead, part of the rewarding unit or reunion fantasy was projected not back on the mother but on the landscape so that in a fantasy merger with the landscape he would be able to feel the feelings of ecstacy and wonder and gratification that he probably felt earlier in life on the basis of a symbiotic fantasy with the mother. This would help to explain the lush, outsized grandiose feelings and styles of expression he always used to describe the landscape—as though for him it represented a gratifying symbiotic mother.

He was also to become rhapsodic in his feelings and expressions about trains, about boats, cars, all forms of conveyance. These feelings were no doubt romanticisms of his need to distance from the object in order to deal with his fear of loss of the self—leaving one place of commitment or trap for an apparent openness which appeared like an escape to freedom. He was always able to deny that what lay at the end of the journey was not freedom and escape but the same abandonment depression which now required additional defenses. He also could deny that the trap was internal, not external, and that the travel only changed the scenery, not the problem.

Youth (Ages 12 to 25)

In my treatment experience with borderline patients, life never seems to cooperate in that the patients seem to be exposed to a heavy dose of the operation of Murphy's Law—whatever bad can happen will happen. Thomas Wolfe's life is an exception in that he was extraordinarily fortunate in meeting and having relationships with adults who had upstanding characters and were genuinely interested in his career. No manipulators or scoundrels used or abused him. He received loyal, steadfast support from people who were an almost perfect fit for the emergence of his creative self.

The first was his teacher, Mrs. Roberts, at the North Masters School which he attended from age 12 to 16. She saw a composition of his without ever having seen or heard of him, but when she read his paper she felt that this "was a genius." She taught him composition, history and English literature and was the first to acknowledge his creative self and to encourage him to express it.

He has written (1936): "It was through her that I first developed a taste for good literature which opened up a shining eldorado for me. She was much more than a mere teacher. Her influence was 'inestimable' in almost every particular in my life and thought. I was groping like a blind sea thing with no eyes and a thousand feelers toward life, toward beauty and order and then I found her. You mother of my spirit who fed me with light. Do you think that I have forgotten? Do you think I ever will."

Mrs. Roberts' behavior resonated with his rewarding unit symbiotic fantasy. He established his symbiotic dependency on her, felt approved of and loved. His depression was relieved and his energies were refueled. Her acknowledgment of his creative self helped him to activate it and support the activity of writing.

In high school Tom had grown immensely to 6'5" and was described as being so garrulous that his conversation flowed "like an elemental flood." The writing as an activity was then reinforced by reality when he won the bronze medal offered by a magazine for the best essay written at the North State School. The inborn talent for words was now linked to the act of writing but, matters of learning and craft aside, a crucial psychological dimension was still lacking and it would be a long time before he would find it and thereby gain access to his creative source and activate his real self.

Tom graduated at 16 and wanted to go to Princeton, but his father refused to support it. Instead, he went off to the University of North Carolina, his first trip away from home. At the same time his father developed an illness from which he would eventually die. The first year at college—i.e., on his own—was extremely painful as he was depressed and lived completely alone. His lack of social skills made him isolated, and he spent much of his time mooning over his first love affair with an obviously unavailable young woman who was about to be married. In his second year he won a position on the college paper and his life turned around. He joined everything, was initiated into fraternities, and began to get more and more external reinforcement for his writing. He was editor of the college magazine and associate editor of another magazine in which his poetry and stories appeared. He found another mentor, Professor Greenlaw, upon whom to fasten his symbiotic projection and learned from him much about Elizabethan literature.

In the summer of 1918, after his successful sophomore year, instead of returning home he went to Norfolk to try to work. The summer was "filled with terror and hunger," for he was exposed to abandonment depression as he was now on his own—roaming the streets, drinking, a harbinger of the distancing pattern that was to form one of the main stereotypical themes of his life.

In his junior year his beloved brother Ben, who had always urged him to get away from home, died of pneumonia with some suspicion that it was related to the fact that the mother did not take proper care of him. Ben had championed Tom so Tom always referred to his death as the most tragic experience of his entire life. Ben had always urged Tom to get away and now, with Ben's death, he began to realize himself that he should. He described his mother from this vantage point in *Look Homeward Angel* (1929): "She sat before the fire with hands folded, reliving a past of tenderness and love that *had never been*. And as the wind howled in the bleak street and she wove a thousand fables of that lost and bitter spirit the bright and stricken thing in the boy twisted about in horror looking for escape from the house of death. No more, no more, it said. You are alone now. You are lost. Go and find yourself, lost boy, beyond the hills" (Nowell, 1960, p. 44).

His guilt overcomes him as he says: "I can't go now because her face is so white, her forehead so broad and high, with the black hair drawn back from it and when she sat there at the bed she looked like a little child. I can't go now and leave her here alone. She is alone, the voice said, and so are you. You must escape or you will die. It is all like death. She fed me her breast, I slept in the same bed with her, she took me on her trips, all of that is over now and each time it was like a death.

"And like a life, the voice said to him, and each time that you die you will be born again and you will die a hundred times before you become a man. I can't, I can't. Not now, later, more slowly. No, now, it said. I'm afraid, I have nowhere to go. You must find a place it said. I am lost. You must hunt for yourself it said.

"Eugene heard the whine of the bleak wind of the house that he must leave and the voice of Eliza calling up from the past the beautiful lost things that never happened."

Mother is tempting him and trying to seduce him with fantasies of reunion: "And I said, 'Why, what on earth boy, you want to dress up warm around your neck or you'll catch a death of cold.' Eugene caught at his throat and lunged for the door. Here boy, where are you going, said Eliza looking up quickly. I've got to go, he said, I've got to get away from here. Then he saw the fear in her eyes and the grave troubled child stare. He rushed to her as she sat and grasped her hand. She held it tightly and laid her face against his arm. Don't go yet she said. You've all your life ahead of you. Stay with me a day or two. Yes, mamma he said falling to his knees. Yes, mamma. He hugged her frantically. God bless you mamma, it's all right and she wept bitterly. I'm an old woman she said and one by one I've lost you all. He's dead now and I never got to know him. Don't leave me son yet. You are the only one who's left. You are my baby. Don't go, don't go. She laid her white face against his sleeve. It's not hard to go he thought but when can we forget."

In this passage from *Look Homeward Angel*, Wolfe described his perception, at the time of his brother's death, of the withdrawing-unit object representation of the mother that lay beneath the rewarding-unit fantasies. He struggled in fright to leave, describing how the mother clung to him and his guilt about leaving her.

He returned to North Carolina after the death of his father and again was successful in all of his literary activities, winning a prize for an essay on philosophy. He came under the influence of Frederick H. Koch, who had begun to organize the Carolina Playmakers, and he became intensely involved and wrote a number of plays. His writing efforts again received acknowledgment and reinforcement from the environment.

In spite of this, as graduation time came, he was very confused about what he wanted to do. He could not yet identify and activate his real self. It was the same when he had finished high school: "The desire to write which had been stronger in all my days in high school grew stronger still. I was still thinking of becoming a lawyer or a newspaper man, never daring to believe I could seriously become a writer" (1936, p. 30).

This ambiguity was no clearer at the end of college. Since it seemed so clear that his pathway had to do with writing, why was he not able to identify it further? I believe it was because of his difficulty in identifying and articulating the individuative wishes of his real self, on the one hand, and on the other because his writing was still motivated by his defensive self. In other words, he wrote to please the idealized omnipotent objects such as Professor Koch rather than to express his real self. It took him a long time to discover that playwriting was not an appropriate métier for him. Only then could he gain access to the great generator and reservoir of his creative talent. It had to remain hidden, defended against, because of his continued intrapsychic and external dependence on his mother.

Finishing college and ostensibly having to be on his own potentiated and crystallized his underlying psychological dilemma. He was unable to activate his real self, identify what he wanted, and implement it. However, he realized that he could no longer cling to his mother and he wished to distance himself from her by escaping. This all became articulated in his fantasy that the North would provide the escape, would be the omnipotent maternal object that would acknowledge his real self and enable him to activate and fulfill it.

Tom gradually developed the idea of doing further graduate study in playwriting at Harvard under Professor George Baker. This second geographic move was a distancing phenomena to deal with his fear of loss of self if he stayed in the web and trap of his relationship with his mother in Asheville.

In his first year at Harvard he was surrounded by friends, taken care of by an uncle (again, as so often happened in his life, he found someone else to take care of him), and he idealized and worshipped his new symbiotic omnipotent object, Professor Baker. "I worshipped him for almost a year. He was the great man, the prophet, the infinitely wise and strong and gentle spirit who knew all, had seen all and could solve all problems by a word, release us of all the anguish, grief and error of our lives by a wave of his benevolent hand" (Nowell, 1960, p. 52). And he flung himself into his work as a dramatist and playwright guided by Baker.

Tom's hunger for reading continued and he took in all that the library could offer, as well as making lists, endless, endless lists. When the term closed and the other students went home, he was left to stay on alone. This precipitated, as it had years ago in Norfolk, his abandonment depression. He suffered from one of those astounding suspensions of will which were to be frequent in his life. For six weeks he found himself powerless to perform a single act to relieve himself from the limbo, a terrible inaction in which his life was held. He was very lonely and completely broke, but he did not dare go home for fear that he would not be allowed to come back in the fall—and also for fear that he would lose his sense of self.

He managed to persuade his reluctant mother to grudgingly support a second year at Harvard. At the beginning of that year in 1921 his father died. Loss of his father reinforced his abandonment depression and redoubled his search to find his real self. He returned to Harvard for a third year with the workshop 47 Group—Professor George Baker's playwriting course. "I lived in a kind of dream, in a radiance, drunken with joy and power" (Nowell, 1960, p. 51). However, struggle as he might, his plays were not a success. Playwriting was not his medium. The plays were too long, with too many characters and scenes, and he was unable to cut them down. However, Professor Baker, his latest symbiotic god, kept encouraging him.

He finally realized that his plays were not "working" and that playwriting was not for him. He decided that he would have to become a teacher. Even at this point, age 24, with all of the writing he had done and all the ability he had shown, it had not yet occurred to him to write novels—to tap the generator and reservoir.

The disillusionment with his idealized symbiotic god was now repeated with Baker as he projected the withdrawing unit back on his former symbiotic god. He wrote to Mrs. Roberts: "I began to understand how bitter a draught it was that Professor Baker was an excellent friend, a true critic but a bad counselor. I knew from that time on that the disposition of my life was mainly in my own hands" (Nowell, 1960, p. 72). In *Of Time and the River* (1935) he wrote: "And then I saw that half the man was sawdust, that he was lacking in warmth and greatness and humanity, unable to see the genuine quality in a man and he lavished his benefits on buffoons, feeble weaklings, and let most of the good people (*i.e., Tom Wolfe*), the people with a spark of life, go to hell."

In defeat Tom Wolfe turned from playwriting to enter the field of teaching with as little enthusiasm as possible. Although he did not have any great desire to teach, his new position had the advantage of placing him on his own in all ways, free from his family, so that he had to come to grips with his underlying problems once and for all.

He wrote in *The Story of a Novel* (1936): "With me this period was a time of stress and torment for I had now committed myself utterly, there was no going back. No compromise and my position was a desperate one. I pulled up my roots bodily, broken almost utterly away from my old life, from my family, my native town, my earlier associations (*i.e., his old defenses*). There was nothing now for me except myself and my work. Nothing beyond myself that could help me. My strength would be in myself. I had to pull it from myself. If I could not there would be no hope."

As might have been expected, being on his own precipitated his depression and his withdrawing unit fantasies. He was tortured constantly by the thought of his inadequacy and ignorance as a teacher and by the horrible fear that his incompetence would be discovered and that he would be fired.

In desperation but determined to manage, he worked himself to the bone night and day, containing his loneliness and desolation. He learned his job and found his life again. This was the first activation of his real self. The work was so demanding that he was unable to write: "My life is like water which has passed the mill. It turns no wheel. The great play is yet unwritten, the great novel beats with futile hands against the portals of my brain. There is not time. If I had but a hundred years there might be some realization of my dream but I shall not live so long" (Nowell, 1960, p. 80). The major saving grace of the teaching job was that he was allowed to have the fall term off so that he could travel to Europe, which he believed was a necessary part of his education as a writer.

The next chapter describes how the long struggle came to fruition and fulfillment.

CHAPTER X

Thomas Wolfe's Quest
for a Real Self—
Partial Fulfillment

On the brink of this next, most dramatic and important turning point of Thomas Wolfe's life, let us pause for a moment to consider the personality of this now fully grown young man.

PERSONALITY*

He was 6'5" tall, garrulous, and spoke with a lisp. He had dramatic mood swings from states of euphoria to the blackest of depression. Though physically awkward and without conventional social skills, he had the capacity to draw other people into providing for him what he was unable to do for himself. In addition to his few symbiotic attachments, over the years he amassed an extraordinary range of people throughout western Europe and the United States who on his travels were prepared to be his

---

*This section is based on Nowell (1960).

150

caretaker—as long as the relationship was not longstanding and intimate, he was able to manage it.

His father's message that adult responsibility for self and others leads only to depression and resentment was well learned by Tom. He always found someone else to do it for him. Was he acting out helplessness to evoke others to resonate with his rewarding unit defense?

He was bright, had a good sense of humor, loved all sorts of conveyances, boats, trains, was interested in baseball, was suspicious of others which sometimes made him accuse even his best friends "of betraying" him when in the depths of his depression his fear of loss of self and withdrawing unit got the better of him. He was impulsive and basically undisciplined except when it came to his work, where he could discipline himself to work long hours without letup.

From the perspective of the development of the real self he showed marked impairment, with a minimal capacity for mature intimacy. By the age of 24 he had had no long-term relationships with women although he was sexually attracted to them and had many short-term sexual encounters. He had little capacity for autonomy, his life to date and thereafter revolving around intense symbiotic attachments. In addition, most notable was his impairment of what could be called the responsible caretaking functions of the real self. Either he did not have much of this capacity or he was flagrantly acting out helplessness. He was completely inattentive to whether or not he had bathed or had a haircut, and wore the same clothes until they fell off his body. It has been said that when he undressed he simply took his clothes off and left them on the floor where they lay.

Tom had a chronic inability to keep track of time and was late to meetings, to classes, with work assignments, etc. He was unable to keep track of his belongings, losing various clothes, manuscripts, checks. He had difficulty managing his money. In other words, he had difficulty in the organizing and synthesizing functions based on reality perception of the real self. He was unable to organize and shape his writing in order to make it meet the demands of reality so that it could be published. What we see, then, is the ego defects of his developmental arrest: poor reality perception, weak impulse control, little frustration tolerance, and vague ego boundaries. On the other hand, he had an enormous appetite for knowledge, tremendous persistence in pursuing his own interests and, as we shall see, paradoxically the courage and strength to discipline himself to create the conditions that made it possible for his creativity and talents to be fulfilled.

WRITING, CREATIVITY AND ALINE BERNSTEIN

His first trip to Europe was a notable turning point in Tom's life, but it began badly. He was now alone, on his own, and his abandonment depression again surfaced as it had at Norfolk and Harvard when he was on his own. Again he required additional acting-out defenses such as drinking and restless wandering, so that for months the trip was a disaster.

Despite his grimly sitting down to write, after a few impatient fragmentary beginnings, he would brusquely toss them aside. He was having enormous difficulty activating his talent and creativity on his own because of his abandonment depression. But he did not give up, he kept at it, and suddenly he began to write, as he put it, "like a madman, tranced in a hypnosis by whose fatal and insatiated compulsions he was forced without will to act. The words were wrung out of him in a kind of bloody sweat. He wrote them with his heart, his brain, his sweat, his guts, his blood, his spirit. They were wrenched out of the last secret source and substance of his life and in them was packed the whole image of his bitter homelessness, his intolerable desire, his mad longing for return. They were all there without coherence, scheme or reason. The huge single and incomparable substance of America" (Nowell, 1960, pp. 94-95).

Through this trip to Europe he had used physical distance to put himself in a place where he was alone on his own, away from his usual supports. His depression and loneliness surfaced, he managed to control his usual acting-out defenses and in a titanic battle activated the creative part of his real self to overcome the regressive defenses. He wrote without purpose or direction. He described it as "finding his own, i.e., America." I think what he meant was that for him America was his childhood memories of Asheville and mother.

The trip interrupted his clinging and rewarding unit defenses and released his abandonment depression, making it impossible for him to activate his real self and write as he sought defense through acting out. When he controlled the acting out, the abandonment depression was now channeled into and found release in his writing. It was a profoundly courageous and disciplined act by an otherwise undisciplined person. However, he still could not further acknowledge and define his creative purpose without a substitute maternal object and again fate cooperated with his needs.

On the trip home from this dramatic discovery of the generator and reservoir of his writing talent, he meets Aline Bernstein on the boat and they fall madly in love. He wrote: "From that moment on he never was again to lose her utterly, never to wholly repossess unto himself the lonely wild integrity of youth which had been his as he was impaled upon the knife of love. After all the blind, tormented wanderings of youth that woman would become his heart's center, the target of his life, the image of immortal oneness that again collected him to one and hurled the whole collective passion, power and might that was one life into the blazing certitude, the immortal governance and unity of love" (Nowell, 1960, p. 96).

Aline now performed the functions for Wolfe that he was unable to perform for himself and thereby fulfilled the remaining conditions necessary to unleash the mighty engine of his creativity. She was 20 years older than Wolfe, a success in her own right as a stage designer in the theater, and a person of grit, determination and executive capacity. She assumed the caretaking functions he had such difficulty with, including supporting him financially as his mother had before.

Wolfe now transferred his symbiotic dependence from his mother to Aline in their love relationship. This transfer provided a very essential and important dynamic. Wolfe had now found 'another superior being, another image of strength and wisdom external to his need and superior to his hunger to which the belief and power of his own life could be united" (Nowell, 1960, p. 102).

Incidentally, in describing his relationship with her he reveals his underlying dilemma (1929): "The only home a man ever has on earth, the only moment when he escapes from the prisms of loneliness is when he enters into the heart of another person. In all the enormous darkness of living and dying I see these brave little lights go up, the only hope and reason for it all." But he called it love: "I believe in love and in its power to redeem and save our lives. I believe in the loved one, the redeemer, the savior." The phrase "the prison of loneliness" expresses for Wolfe the feeling that the loneliness of being on his own was so powerful that it overrode and almost eliminated the pleasure.

Aline provided two other essential functions: she helped him once and for all to lay aside the notion that he was a playwright, that his style with its abundance of scenes and characters and variety of places and people would ever fit the stage. In addition, she not only acknowledged and encouraged his writing but also was quite sympathetic to the deprivations of his childhood and youth as he expressed them. She acknowledged these key aspects of his real self.

Just prior to meeting Aline, Wolfe had controlled his acting-out defenses and had gotten in touch with the emergence of his real creative self in his writing, albeit blindly, stumblingly and without purpose or direction. Her acknowledgment, encouragement and support reinforced the emergence of his real self and helped to give it purpose and direction, but beyond that, the transfer of the symbiotic attachment from his mother to Aline provided an even more important dynamic that made it possible for him to get in touch with the reservoir of his creative real self.

In order to understand this dynamic, it is necessary to describe briefly what happens in psychotherapy to borderline patients with a similar type of symbiotic dependency upon the mother. In the beginning of treatment, the patient denies his negative feelings of anger, disappointment and disillusionment at the mother's scapegoating in order to support his rewarding unit defenses and relieve his separation anxiety and abandonment depression. He is afraid that if he expresses them he will be exposed to that anxiety and depression. At the same time, he is afraid that if he expresses them to the mother she will withdraw. Therefore, these feelings and the memories attached to them are defended against by splitting, avoidance, denial and projection, and are unavailable to the patient.

Wolfe had been unable to get in touch with the enormous generator and reservoir of his creativity—his childhood memories with their anger, their disillusionment and all the negatives —because to do so would have threatened his dependent relationship with his mother. When he transferred his dependency from his mother to Aline—in other words, when the rewarding unit projection shifted from his mother to Aline—he was now freed to take the withdrawing unit projection which he had heretofore projected on other people and place it back on his mother without the same threat of abandonment, since he was now dependent upon Aline. This freed him to get in touch with "all the incidents he could remember from his youth." This was the great generator and reservoir of his creative talent that had to be tapped in order to fulfill that talent, as well as to fulfill the expression of the creativity of his real self.

To summarize the conditions required for the unleashing of the creativity of his real self: (1) the symbiotic attachment to a maternal object—Aline—who does not require him to be her possession; on the contrary, she supports and encourages the emergence of his real creative self and also performs the necessary caretaking functions for him that he is unable to perform; (2) Thomas Wolfe himself, controlling his acting-out defenses against the abandonment depression; (3) generally being alone in a foreign place and being able to deal with his fear of engulfment and loss of self because of the symbiotic union with Aline.

The conditions I have just outlined are strikingly similar to the conditions that occur in psychoanalytic psychotherapy of a borderline patient that enable the patient to work through his abandonment depression so that his real self can emerge: a real therapeutic alliance in which the therapist is supportive and acknowledging of the patient's real self; control of the patient's clinging and distancing defenses against the abandonment depression; emergence of the impaired real self and the abandonment depression with all its memories from the past. This is an automatic process that occurs if the defenses are controlled.

Whenever the defenses are interrupted, the force of the abandonment depression makes the affects and their associations flow like a river. The therapist's only task is to remove whatever additional obstacles of resistance appear to impede the flow of the river. In sum, the emotional force of the abandonment depression after the defenses are interrupted drives the treatment.

The patient is not in charge of the process except to the degree that he controls his defenses. The force then inevitably finds its way into the sessions through memories and the discharge of the rage and depression associated with these memories. Patients will speak of being "in the grip of a power" or of being the bystander at a process, often of being inundated and overwhelmed by the intensity and force of these feelings and associated memories.

This is exactly how Thomas Wolfe (1936) described his creative writing process or the emergence of his real self:

> It was a storm, a flood, a river, an elemental force which had to find release and if energy of this kind is not used it keeps boiling over and is given no way out. It will eventually destroy and smother the person who has it. I wrote about things that I had known, the immediate life and experience that had been familiar to me in my childhood. I had somehow recovered innocence, I have written it almost with a child's heart, it has come from me with a child's wonder and my pages are engraved not only with what is simple and plain but with monstrous evil as if the Devil were speaking with a child's tongue. The great fish though sealed with evil, horribly incandescent hoary with elvish light, have swum upwards. (Nowell, 1960, p. 105).

All borderline patients in psychotherapy are regularly astonished at the flood of their negative perceptions of their childhood experience. At the outset Wolfe did not realize that his childhood memories would continue to "swim upwards" and keep the book (1929) coming from him for almost two more years until it utterly exhausted him. It reached 350,000 words, three times the length of the average novel.

His creative real self was now in full sway. He had to

> pour it out, boil it out, flood it out until he realized himself through a process of torrential production. He could remember all that people said or did from his childhood, but as he tried to set it down his memory opened up enormous vistas and associations going from depth to limitless depth until the simplest incident conjured up a buried increment of experience and he was overwhelmed by this process of discovery and revelation that would have broken the strength and used up the lives of a regiment of men. (Nowell, 1960, p. 106)

These same characteristics apply to the working-through process in psychotherapy: the innocence of childhood and the regaining of enormous floods of memories that have previously been held in restraint by the need for defense.

He wrote:

> The life of Paris aroused all the old feelings of homelessness, rootlessness and loneliness which I'd always felt there. I felt this great homesickness and I really believe that from this emotion, this constant and almost intolerable effort of memory and desire, the material and structure of the books I now began to write were derived. The quality of my memory is characterized I believe in a more than ordinary degree by the intensity of its sense impressions. Its power to evoke and bring back the odors, sounds, colors, shapes and feel of things with concrete vividness. My memory was at work night and day in a way that at first I could neither check nor control and it swarmed unbidden in the stream of blazing pageantry across my mind with a million forms and substances of the life that I had left which was my own America. (Nowell, 1960, p. 168)

He then described the process:

> I would be sitting for example on the terrace of a cafe watching the flashing play of life before me on the Avenue de l'Opéra

and suddenly I would remember the iron railing that goes along the boardwalk at Atlantic City. I could see it instantly just the way it was, the heavy iron pipe, its raw galvanized look, the way the joints were fitted together, it was so vivid and concrete I could feel my hand upon it and know the exact dimensions. And suddenly I would realize that I had not seen anything. Any railing that looked like this in Europe and this utterly familiar common thing would suddenly be revealed to me with all the wonder with which we discover a thing which we have seen all our life and have never known before.

Again, it would be an American street with all its jumble of a thousand ugly architectures. I would sit there looking at the Avenue de l'Opéra and my life would ache with the whole memory of it, the desire to see it again, somehow to find a word for it, a language that would tell its shape, its color, the way we have all known and felt and seen it and when I understood this thing I saw that I must find for myself the tongue to utter what I know but could not say and from the moment of that discovery the line and purpose of my life was shaped. The ends towards which every energy of my life and talent would be henceforth directed was in such a way as this defined. (p. 169)

I think Wolfe is referring here to the psychological purpose of his writing which contrasts with the purpose of the working-through process in treatment. The purpose of this process is to discharge the painful feelings of loss associated with the abandonment depression in order to free the real self from this anchor so that it can separate from the object, emerge and become autonomous and assume its capacities. Since Wolfe was not in treatment, this was not possible for him. The psychological purpose of his writing was to deal with all these painful feelings of loss associated with his abandonment depression by recapturing them and memorializing them forever in writing so that they would never be lost again. In this process, he managed to activate and consolidate the creative aspect of his real self, but the remaining capacities of the self were still impaired.

Wolfe describes another example of how the abandonment depression motivated his writing (1936):

It seemed that I had inside me swelling and gathering all the time a huge black cloud and this cloud was loaded with electricity, pregnant, crested with a kind of hurricane violence that could not be held in check much longer. The moment was approaching fast when it must break while all I can say is that the storm did break. I cannot really say the book was written, it was something that took hold of me and possessed me and before I was done with it, it seemed to me that it had done for me. It was exactly as if this great black storm cloud had opened up and mid flashes of lightning was pouring from its depth a torrential and ungovernable flood. (Nowell, 1960, p. 172)

He further described what sounds like free association: "I wrote not only the concrete material record of man's ordered memory but all of the things he scarcely dares to think he has remembered, all the flicks and darts of haunting lights that flash across the mind of man that will return unbidden at an unexpected moment, a voice once heard, a face that vanished, the way the sunlight came and went, the rustling of a leaf upon a bough, a stone, a leaf, a door."

My idea that his psychological purpose was to capture and engrave these memories forever is reinforced by Wolfe's (1936) comment: "My job was to dig it up, get it down, somehow record it, transform it into the objective record of manuscript even upon thousands and thousands of pages that would never be printed and no reader would ever see, that would never be framed into the sequence of a narrative. At any rate now would be there at last upon the record worth all the labor of the effort just so long as I could get it down, get it down" (Nowell, 1960, p. 194).

Nowell (1960) describes it as follows: "He simply poured out whatever happened to be uppermost in his mind in separate chunks of first person narrative regardless of chronology or order and with no connective material" (p. 194).

As Perkins wrote in 1935 (Nowell, 1960), "No book was ever written in such an extraordinary fashion. It started almost backwards and it came in sections that seemed to have no relation to each other and yet it still did have a kind of unity in the mind of the author even at the beginning" (p. 194). Wolfe was too completely absorbed in his "enormous task of excavation" to think of arranging his material as a book. Wolfe said,

> Having had this thing within me it was in no way possible for me to reason it out of me no matter how cogently my reason worked against it. The only way I could meet it was to meet it squarely, not with reason but with life. The only way I could get it out of me was to live it out of me and that is what I did.

True to form, whenever he was distracted from his creative work he would get into a depression, brood and drink and pace the streets all night, and telephone his friends to accuse them of betraying him. When he was not dealing with his abandonment depression through the discharge involved in writing, it overwhelmed him and he required defenses of drinking and attacking his friends. He elaborated further: "If I can only keep on writing everything will be all right." He meant it not only for the sake of his literary output but also for his peace of mind. Basically, his whole daily life was governed by his need to write.

As he struggled to find his real creative self in his real life and to free himself from his symbiotic fixation to his mother, he struggled with *Of Time and the River* (1935). He thought first of calling it "The Building of a Wall" (Nowell, 1960) to symbolize the struggle of the hero to find "an essential isolation, a creative solitude, a secret life"—in my view a real creative self. He described the theme of the book as "consisting of two essential movements, one outward and one downward. The outward movement describes the effort of the youth for release, freedom and loneliness in new lands." For Thomas Wolfe freedom was always associated with loneliness, not with fulfillment. "The downward movement is represented by constant excavation into the buried life of a group of people and describes the cyclic curve of a family's life, genesis, union, decay and dissolution." In my judgment, it's a story of the struggle to free himself from his symbiotic dependence on the mother and to activate his real self.

The book (1935) now almost completed, the symbiotic intensity and closeness of the relationship with Aline, who was old enough to be his mother and functioned too much like a mother for him in every way, began to exacerbate and stimulate his fear of engulfment and loss of self. The kernel of this fear was that if he allowed the continuation of the symbiotic fusion with the object he would lose himself, meaning his creativity and his capacity to write. It seems to me that this is the ultimate reason why he had to separate from Aline, as he did later from Perkins, although obviously there were additional reasons. However, he was only dimly aware of his fear of engulfment and loss of self.

To promote his separation from Aline, he returned to Europe. Again his abandonment depression surfaced and he defended as usual through wandering, through drinking, through sexual acting out, and was unable to write. His description in his diary (Nowell, 1960) of his depression is a telling one and resembles the themes described by many of my adolescent patients:

> Today has been a horrible one. I was able to sleep only the most diseased and distressed sleep, the worst sort of American in Europe sleep and I got sick with the shakes, the day was the most horrible European sort, something that passes understanding. The wet heavy air that deadens the soul, puts a lump of indigestible lead in the solar plexus, depresses and fatigues the flesh until one seems to lift himself leadenly through the thick, wet, steaming air. With this a terrible kind of fear, an excitement that is without hope, that awaits only the news of some further grief, failure or humiliation and torture. A lassitude that enters the soul and makes one hope for better things and better work tomorrow but hope without belief or conviction. (Nowell, 1960, p. 167)

He finally became disgusted with his self-destructive behavior and "sets to work" where he described his motive as "an abysmal homesickness for America."

In the struggle to separate from Aline, he hypocritically placed the responsibility on her and on her friends who were saying he should leave. He said (Nowell, 1960): "I have never betrayed or deserted anyone. In the end, if anyone gets betrayed or deserted, it will be me" (p. 118). He also spoke of the inescapable conviction that he must be free to live and work alone. In other words, he must be free of his fears of loss of self which are prompted not by the other person but by the intensity of his own symbiotic wishes. One could reword that statement as follows: He must be alone to be free to work, i.e., he must be free from his fears of loss of self.

The symbiotic fantasy carries with it a notion of exclusive possession of the object. Wolfe's projection of this on Aline led to frequent paranoid outbursts of jealousy about her relationships with other men, for which there evidently was no basis at all in fact. This contributed to the demise of the relationship.

He would accuse her of betraying him and then say that her betrayal was the reason he had to leave her. For example, in describing his character in *The Web and the Rock* (1937) he said,

> Perhaps, although he did not know it, there was destruction in him too, for what he loved and got his hands on he squeezed dry and it could not be otherwise for him. It was something that came from nature, from memory, from inheritance, from the blazing images of youth, from something outside of him and external to him, yet within him that drove him forever and that he could not help. (Nowell, 1960, p. 116)

I think he is referring here again to his basic, lifelong dilemma, his need to idealize the omnipotent object and take from it all nourishment, squeezing it dry in hope of getting the acknowledgment of his real self so that he could find, activate and fulfill it. This, of course, was a fantasy which always ended in disillusionment and disappointment. He described it further (Nowell, 1960):

> Love made me mad and brought me down to the level of the beast. I have wasted everything most precious (speaking to Aline) paramountly yourself and made a wreck of everything I want to make beautiful. I do not know the reason for it. It seems to me that the people who lose all reason in this world are the people who try most desperately to find it. I know I have always been after the reason of things. I am now more than ever. My brain is weary and wants rest and cannot get it.

It is like something that hunts round and round inside an iron solder trying to find some way out when there is none. We can do nothing until we know our limits and I have never found mine. I don't know what they are and at present I am spiritually a growling worm wondering why some useful catastrophe cannot erase this constructiveless, lightless and nothingless life. (p. 125)

THE PERKINS PERIOD

As Wolfe was attempting to free himself from what he saw as the engulfing tentacles of Aline Bernstein, life again came to his aid by supplying a substitute object, his editor, Maxwell Perkins, who came to perform the same functions for Wolfe, even psychologically, that Aline had. Wolfe developed the same symbiotic dependency on Perkins that he had had on Aline. Beyond that, Perkins performed not only the caretaking functions but also, of course, the organizing and synthesizing functions for Wolfe's work. It appears to have been a mutually symbiotic relationship: Wolfe saw Perkins as this omnipotent object, wiser, superior, external to himself, that could provide him with the support and nourishment that he required, whereas Perkins saw Wolfe, I suspect, as his alter ego, as the author he had always wanted to be, and derived great satisfaction from helping Wolfe fulfill his creativity.

Wolfe said about Perkins (Nowell, 1960) "For the first time in my life I was getting criticism I could really use. The scenes he wanted to cut or change were the least essential and least interesting; all the scenes I had thought too coarse, vulgar, profane or obscene for publication he forbade me to touch save for a word or two" (p. 132). This was acknowledgment of his creative real self to a fare-thee-well and Wolfe described himself as being "drunk with glory."

Wolfe elaborated on the symbiotic nature of the relationship as follows (Nowell, 1960):

You are now mixed with my book in such a way that I can never separate the two of you. I can no longer think clearly of the time I wrote it but rather of the time when you first talked to me about it and when you worked through it. You have done what I had ceased to believe one person could do for another. You have created liberty and hope for me. Young men sometimes believe in the existence of heroic figures, stronger and wiser than themselves to whom they can turn for an answer to all their vexation and grief. Later they must discover that such answers have to come out of their own hearts. The powerful desire to believe in such figures persists. You are for me such a figure. You are one of the rocks to which my life is anchored. (p. 157)

In retrospect, one would be tempted to say at this point, as the relationship deepened, beware of the fear of loss of self.

When *Look Homewood Angel* (1929) was published and successful, Wolfe exulted in this ultimate acknowledgment of his real creative self by his environment. But since the book was autobiographical, it caused an enormous critical furor in his hometown. His former mentor, Mrs. Roberts, his family and the townspeople were described in such exact detail that he was forced to cut himself off from the town for the next seven years. Wolfe rationalized this use of other people by saying (Nowell, 1960): "No one in the end ever got hurt by a great book or if he did it was paltry and temporary compared to the amounts of good that was conferred" (p. 363). I imagine he meant the good of humanity. It was far easier for him who required the material to see it that way than for the people who were hurt by it.

Wolfe continued to write, spent a great deal of time with Perkins, who became his mentor, his savior, his advisor, his father-confessor, and continued to travel to Europe where he would repeat the same cycle: distancing to be alone, depression, acting-out defenses, control of the acting out, the return of the flood of memories, and return to writing. However, he was unable to organize the vast amount of material. Finally Perkins organized it for him and it became *Of Time and the River* (1935).

Wolfe wished to acknowledge Perkins' contribution. Perkins tried to dissuade him but finally Wolfe did so in a speech which opened a whole barrage of accusations that the author did not write his own book, that it was essentially a symbiotic production. In all probability Wolfe's fear of loss of self in the closeness with Perkins was already mounting and this accusation became the final straw which impelled him to leave Perkins as he had Bernstein. He again became disillusioned and disappointed, projected his withdrawing unit upon the undeserving Perkins, accused him of betrayal, and finally severed the relationship although he left Perkins as the executor of his will and estate.

His projections at this point would become almost paranoid. He felt overwhelmed with resentment. He accused Perkins of everything from being "just a good but timid man" to trying to destroy him (shades of Professor Baker and Aline Bernstein). He said to him:

> Are you the man I trusted and reverenced above all else in the world, trying for some mad reason I cannot guess to destroy me? Is it really the end? I fear desperately we have reached the end. It is also tragically sad and, as for that powerful magnificent talent I had, in the name of God is that to be lost entirely, destroyed under the repeated assaults and criminalities of this blackmail society in which we live? Now I know what happens to the artist in America. (Nowell, 1960, p. 36)

Here he is projecting his fear of loss of self upon Perkins, Scribners (the publisher), and society. It is not that his symbiotic wishes threaten to destroy his self and his creativity, but rather that they are out to destroy him. Nowell (1960) wrote:

> He was so obsessed with the desire for freedom that he could talk of nothing else till Perkins in exasperation once exclaimed, 'All right, if you must leave Scribners then go ahead and leave but for Heaven's sake don't talk about it any more. Moreover, this resentment against Perkins was so deep that it colored everything he did or said and on one occasion it even brought the two men close to blows. (p. 375)

Another relationship had come full circle. Perkins was no longer the heroic figure, stronger and wiser than himself. Now he had become the enemy (WORU) and was trying, as Wolfe said, "to alter the direction of Wolfe's creative life and therefore he must repulse an enemy lest it make the final and unpardonable intrusion upon the one thing in an artist's life that must be held and kept inviolable" (p. 375)—i.e., the need to preserve his real creative self from engulfment by the object. After an extraordinary amount of vacillation and struggle, he finally parted from Scribners and Perkins.

POST PERKINS

After much vacillation, he hired Edward Asner as his editor. He then went off on his ill-fated trip to see the American West for the first time. Evidently, his feeling of being caught in the web or trapped in the symbiotic bind with America, as well as with Asheville, Bernstein and Perkins, was now at its lowest ebb. But on this trip his impulsiveness and his not taking care of himself were as responsible as anything else for his eventual illness and death. He was drinking whiskey from a bottle and gave the bottle to a friend who had pneumonia. He contracted the pneumonia himself, which precipitated a latent tuberculosis condition in his lungs which resulted in fatal tuberculosis of the brain.

CONCLUSION

This consideration of Thomas Wolfe's creativity is not in any way meant to reduce him to a set of mechanical psychological principles. The reservoir of his talent was his abandonment depression and his childhood memories; the generator was his quest to find a real self. Their becoming linked and expressed by his extraordinary writing ability is one of the mysteries of his talent. Control of his own acting-out defenses and the enduring of his depression by an act of will to liberate the creativity of his real self are, on the psychological level, as remarkable accomplishments as his writings on a literary level.

CHAPTER XI

Discussion and Summary

This chapter discusses some of the objections to the point of view presented in this book, offers some evidence on the issue of fantasy versus reality in the causation of emotional conflicts, and concludes with a summary of the main themes of the book.

PRE-OEDIPAL AND OEDIPAL PERSPECTIVES

This work on the self and its disorders, though it has met with wide acceptance, has also encountered inevitable resistance. Behavior therapists and systems theorists object to its psychoanalytic

167

and developmental emphasis, as do those focused on organic and directive approaches. Those who emphasize the interpersonal here-and-now interaction in family, marital and group therapy also object, for the most part, to the concept of an intrapsychic structure based on crucial early developmental events.

More difficult to understand are the objections that spring from many committed to a psychoanalytic point of view. Why should they object to the concept of the internalization and fixation of early conflicts that later have to be worked out in treatment? I first thought that it might be due to lack of knowledge and experience; when the resistance seemed to go beyond that, I thought it was due to politics or territoriality issues. I finally came to the conclusion, discussed below, that the fundamental objection was based on none of these factors but rather on the inherent nature of the material and the individual's capacity to listen and respond to it.

The conscious rational basis of their objection was that it placed entirely too great an emphasis on preoedipal issues at the cost of classic oedipal and instinctual theoretical notions. Let us examine this issue in more detail.

This conflict between preoedipal and oedipal points of view which began over 70 years ago in the disagreement between Freud and Jung (McGuire, 1974) is as alive today and almost as influential as it was at the time of the split between these two giants.

Experiences with present-day proponents of the oedipal view who have difficulty with this preoedipal material about the self compelled me to review this old titanic battle. These experiences—the present difficulties in perspective and the past conflict between these eminent leaders—suggested another possible cause for the difficulty that went beyond the history of conflict with each of their fathers that occurred with Jung and Freud, and beyond differences in perception of the clinical material. Freud's development was ostensibly free of preoedipal problems and he concentrated his work on the oedipal phase; Jung's life was fraught with preoedipal problems.

One must consider the consequences for personality development and later life adult functioning of the resolution of conflict at various stages of development. Freud and, perhaps, present-day supporters of the oedipal perspective more or less effectively resolved their preoedipal conflicts and developed to and beyond the oedipal phase, in the course of which they lost access to the perception within themselves of the preoedipal aspects of their own emotions. Thus, aspects of their own emotions were closed off as a consequence of resolution of conflicts. This does not necessarily suggest psychopathology, but rather a closing off of access to preoedipal conflicts and emotions as part of the resolution. Therefore, material of a preoedipal nature stimulates what they have closed off and creates anxiety. As a result, they must reject the stimulus in order to maintain their own intrapsychic integrity.

Jung (1953) and those with a preoedipal perspective on the other hand, either had preoedipal pathology (like Jung), which resulted in a great sensitivity to preoedipal material, or resolved their preoedipal conflicts by maintaining access to this aspect of their own emotions. Therefore, they are able to perceive and deal with it in others with comfort and a minimum of anxiety. Thus, those with the oedipal and the preoedipal perspectives are compelled to look at the same clinical evidence through different microscopes. The former feel it as stimulus for which they have no internal resonance; it produces anxiety and therefore must be dismissed. The latter respond with internal resonance and therefore feel acceptance, comfort and familiarity.

An example of this reaction by those with an oedipal view may be seen in the action of one analytic institute which, after three years of study, decided there was no such thing as borderline phenomena and there was no need for alterations in therapeutic technique. It seems to me such wholesale dismissal of the critical evidence without much rational argument or consideration is evidence of the kind of denial that I am suggesting. Beyond that, a recent book written by an oedipal proponent (Fierstein, 1978) reported the treatment of obvious borderline patients without any consideration of the fact that they were borderline. The author ruefully reported that the treatment results were not what was hoped for, yet not once did he identify the key preoedipal psychopathology and therefore make the necessary alterations in technique.

In my experience, those therapists who do not have access to the preoedipal within themselves have extreme difficulty adopting the appropriate therapeutic techniques for work with borderline and narcissistic personality disorder patients, even though their work with neurotic patients can be outstanding.

Therefore, it is well for the therapist making a referral to try to get some idea where the therapist he is referring to stands on this issue. I have seen any number of patients, including many who were candidates at analytic institutes, who had undergone years of classical psychoanalysis, no doubt with analysts who were otherwise quite capable, but preoedipal issues continued to ravage their lives, undealt with, unconfronted. This no longer has to happen. Psychotherapy has more to offer.

THE SEDUCTION HYPOTHESIS AND FANTASY VS. REALITY IN PSYCHOTHERAPY OF DISORDERS OF THE SELF

Freud's famous and dramatic rejection of the seduction hypothesis which led to the discovery of the unconscious and of psychoanalysis had the unfortunate side effect of creating a kind of bias against the role of reality in the production of emotional problems—as if what actually happened was not important, only what the patient perceived or felt happened mattered.

The issue has recently been revived by a book (Masson, 1984) reporting on Freud's correspondence with Fliess. The author argued that Freud had rejected the seduction hypothesis because of personal conflicts—not for scientific reasons. The book has revived the debate as to whether the etiologic input comes from reality or fantasy. Psychotherapeutic work with borderline and narcissistic personality disorders sheds some light on this issue.

The clinical evidence is overwhelming that *both* what happened—reality—and the patient's later intrapsychic elaborations of it—fantasy—matter a great deal. It is rarely, if ever, a case of either reality or fantasy. The evidence of the *actual* or real parental scapegoating of borderline adolescents was overwhelming and consistent. It came first from the histories given by the adolescents and the parents. It was corroborated by observations in therapy with the parents of their great difficulty in separating their own needs from those of their adolescents, as well as of their unawareness of how to parent. These initial findings were further reinforced by the memories of the adolescent as he or she worked through the abandonment depression. The final confirmation was the repetition of the problem—in vivo, so to speak—in joint interviews with the parents. The history of conflicts we had obtained, our observations regarding the parents and adolescents, and the memories of the adolescents regarding "what happened" were corroborated in their repetition in joint interview under direct observation.

Thus we have the combination of reality, i.e., "what happened" and the patient's later fantasy elaborations of "what happened."

SUMMARY

The real self is defined as the sum of the self and object representations intrapsychically and their related affective states. The term is used in a sense that is synonymous with healthy or normal and to emphasize the important conscious reality function of the self. The concept is similar to Winnicott's (1965) concept of the true self with the exception that it adds the important reality component. It is also synonymous with the self-identity aspect of Erikson's (1968) concept of identity. The real self has its own development, its own capacities, its own psychopathology, and requires its own specific therapeutic intervention. It is a parallel partner of and functions in tandem with the ego to the point that they are dual and inseparable.

The real self emerges from the dual symbiotic mother-child unit and develops through the stages of separation/individuation to become separate, whole, and autonomous and to take on its own capacities listed below:

Spontaneity and alertness and aliveness of affect;
Self-entitlement, self-activation, assertion, support;
Acknowledgment of self-activation and maintenance of self-esteem;

Soothing of painful affects;
Continuity of self;
Commitment;
Creativity.

Parental encouragement and support (particularly by the mother) of these unique characteristics of the emerging self in the first three years of life are vital to its development, to its becoming whole and assuming its functions. Failures in this parental function make an important contribution to the failure of the self's development and, therefore, to the production of a narcissistic or borderline personality disorder. Although there has been no hypothesis-testing research to establish this thesis, its validity has been confirmed over and over again by my own clinical work and that of others.

To summarize, the real self functions alongside and with the ego to effectively adapt and defend in order to maintain a continuous source for the autonomous regulation of self esteem, as well as to creatively identify and articulate or express in reality the self's unique or individuative wishes.

In the borderline and narcissistic personality disorders, all the capacities of the real self are impaired to some degree. Unable to use their real self to cope, the borderline and narcissistic patient turns instead to a false defensive self. In the borderline personality disorder, it is a false defensive self based on regressive defenses against the abandonment depression. In the narcissistic personality disorder, it is the defensive self based on grandiose, self-omnipotent object representations and their related defenses.

In psychotherapy, as the abandonment depression is worked through and the real self begins to emerge, it is important for the therapist to add communicative matching to his or her therapeutic technique. As the patient presents new thoughts, interests and activities (expressions of the emerging real self), the therapist discusses the reality aspect of these with the patient. The patient experiences these interventions as an acknowledgment and refueling of the real self, which then impels him or her to pursue the real self with a new sense of spontaneity, entitlement and vigor. The communicative matching technique should be used with empathy, discrimination and attention to appropriate fit with the patient's emotional state. Once the patient's real self has become continuously active, it is important for the therapist to stop the communicative matching since it is no longer necessary and would then produce regression.

How does this process of communicative matching work? To answer this question, we first have to understand the operation of the defense mechanism of identification with the aggressor first reported by Ferenczi (1932) and then by Anna Freud (1937). Both borderline and narcissistic disorder patients, in an effort at mastery of overwhelming terror and helplessness, identify with the aggressor and internalize and institutionalize in their psyche the external drama. However, the affects associated with this internalization are so painful that the patient cannot contain and experience them. Thus, a process of externalization occurs, with projection and acting out in the environment of this now internalized drama in order not to feel it. The price paid in maladaptive behavior and the sacrifice of the real self is denied. Beyond that, the feeling states so externalized are not contained in the patient's psyche and not available in the interview for therapeutic work.

The first goal of the treatment is to help patients achieve containment of these feeling states. With the borderline patient this is done through the therapeutic technique of confrontation of the denial of the maladaptive functions of the defenses. With the narcissistic personality disorder it is carried out through the interpretation of the patient's narcissistic vulnerability. Overcoming the denial and the acting out leads patients to perceive how destructive their defenses are to their own objectives, which in turn leads them to control the externalization which results in the containment of affect—meaning that it is now available in the patients' psyche in the interview for therapeutic work. The working through of this now contained, available painful affect of abandonment depression decreases the negative affective burden on the emerging real self and promotes its emergence. This sets the stage for the use of communicative matching to further potentiate that emergence.

I cannot stress enough that the communicative matching must be done from a therapeutic stance of objectivity and neutrality when the therapeutic alliance is firm or else it will lead to reinforcing the rewarding unit or grandiose self defenses and thereby increase resistance.

The therapist may be tempted to use communicative matching inappropriately to deal with his own countertransference. For example, in once-a-week confrontive psychotherapy with a borderline patient, the limits and frustrations of that level of work might induce the therapist to add communicative matching to deal with his or her own frustration, or a therapist with a narcissistic personality disorder who is having countertransference feelings of boredom or depersonification might use communicative matching to relieve these feelings. These temptations must be identified and resisted or the psychotherapy will falter.

The question arises as to why communicative matching doesn't reinforce the borderline patient's rewarding unit defenses and the narcissistic personality disorder's idealizing transference. The answer is that the communicative matching is directed at the real self and, if integrated, will reinforce the real self, leading to greater anxiety, not greater defense. The therapist is frustrating the rewarding unit and the grandiose self, not reinforcing it.

I believe that the addition of a concept of the self enriches developmental object relations theory and brings it closer to a state of wholeness or completion. In retrospect, it seems that this theory, useful though it was, was nevertheless handicapped by the fact that the theory did not take into account *all* of the problem, i.e., it focused on the depression, the ego defenses, and object relations. The self was overlooked or allowed to languish or lag behind and to benefit only indirectly from the other therapeutic activities. With the new addition presented in this volume, developmental object relations theory now has a *whole* perspective on the problems of the disorders of the self that shows how to give adequate attention to the self as well as the object relations. This rounding out of therapeutic perspective, properly applied, will enhance every therapist's work with his patients.

Bibliography

Adler, A. *The Theory and Practice of Individual Psychology.* New York: Harcourt Brace, 1940.

American Psychiatric Association. *Diagnostic and Statistical Manual of Mental Disorders* (Third Edition). Washington, D.C.: American Psychiatric Association, 1980.

Atwood, G. E. The pursuit of being in the life and thought of Jean Paul Satre. *Psychoanalytic Review,* 70, Summer 1983.

Benedict, R. *The Chrysanthemum and the Word: Patterns of Japanese Culture.* New York: New American Library, 1974. (Originally published 1946.)

Bettelheim, B. *Children of the Dream.* New York: Macmillan, 1969.

Bettelheim, B. *Freud and Man's Soul.* New York: Alfred A. Knopf, 1982.

Bowlby, J. *Attachment and Loss: Vol. 1, Attachment.* New York: Basic Books, 1969.

Chess, S., Thomas, A., & Birch, H. *Temperament and Behavior Problems in Childhood.* New York: New York University Press, 1968.

Cinderella. *The Complete Grimms Fairy Tales.* New York: Random House, 1974.

Cowley, M. Looking for the essential me. *New York Times Book Review,* June 17, 1984.

Doi, T. *The Anatomy of Dependence.* Tokyo, Japan: Kodansha International, 1977.

Eggum, A. *Edvard Munch: Painting, Sketches, and Studies.* New York: Clarkson Potter, 1983.

Erikson, E. *Identity, Youth, and Crisis.* New York: W. W. Norton, 1968, pp. 208-231.

Ferenczi, S. Confusion of tongues between adults and the child (the language of tenderness and the language of passion). Paper presented to the International Psychoanalytic Congress, Wiesbaden, September 1932.

Fierstein, S. K. *Termination in Psychoanalysis*. New York: International Universities Press, 1978.

Freud, A. *The Ego and the Mechanisms of Defense*. London: Hogarth Press, 1937.

Freud, S. The question of lay analysis. In J. Strachey (Ed.), *Standard Edition*, 20:183-258. London: Hogarth Press, 1959.

Freud, S. New introductory lectures on psychoanalysis. Lecture XXXI: The dissection of the psychical personality. In J. Strachey (Ed.), *Standard Edition*, 22:57-80. London: Hogarth Press, 1964.

Hartmann, H. *Ego Psychology and the Problem of Adaptation*. New York: International Universities Press, 1958.

Hartmann, H. Comments on the psychoanalytic theory of the ego. In *Essays on Ego Psychology, Selected Problems in Psychoanalytic Theory*. New York: International Universities Press, 1964, pp. 118-141.

Horney, K. *Our Inner Conflicts*. New York: W. W. Norton, 1946.

Horney, K. *Neurosis and Human Growth*. New York: W. W. Norton, 1950.

Horowitz, M., & Zilber, N. Regressive alterations in the self concept. *American Journal of Psychiatry*, 140 (3), March 1983.

Jahoda, M. Toward a social psychology of mental health. Symposium on the Healthy Personality: Supplement II. Problems of Infancy, Childhood. Transactions of Fourth Conference, March 1950.

Jacobson, E. *The Self and the Object World*. New York: International Universities Press, 1964.

Jung, C. G. Two essays on analytic psychology. In *Collected Works*, 7. New York: Pantheon, 1953.

Jung, C. G. *Memories, Dreams, Reflections*. New York: Pantheon, 1973a.

Jung, C. G. *Letters 1906-1950* (trans. R. F. C. Hull). Princeton: Princeton Press, 1973b.

Kernberg, O. Self, ego, affects, drives. *Journal of the American Psychoanalytic Association*, 30:893-917, 1982.

Kohut, H. *The Analysis of the Self*. New York: International Universities Press, 1971.

Kohut, H. *The Restoration of the Self*. New York: International Universities Press, 1977.

Lasch, C. *The Culture of Narcissism*. New York: Norton, 1978.

Mahler, M. *The Psychological Birth of the Human Infant*. New York: Basic Books, 1975.

Mahler, M., & McDevitt, J. Thoughts on the emergence of the self with particular emphasis on the body self. *Journal of the American Psychoanalytic Association*, 30:827-847, 1982.

Masson, J. *The Assault on Truth*. New York: Farrar, Straus, Giroux, 1984.

Masterson, J. *The Psychiatric Dilemma of Adolescence*. Boston: Little, Brown, 1967.

Masterson, J. *Treatment of the Borderline Adolescent: A Developmental Approach*. New York: John Wiley, 1972; Brunner/Mazel, 1985.

Masterson, J. *Psychotherapy of the Borderline Adult: A Developmental Approach*. New York: Brunner/Mazel, 1976.

Masterson, J., with Costello, J. *From Borderline Adolescent to Functioning Adult: The Test of Time*. New York: Brunner/Mazel, 1980.

Masterson, J. *Narcissistic and Borderline Disorders: An Integrated Developmental Approach*. New York: Brunner/Mazel, 1981.

Masterson, J. *Countertransference and Psychotherapeutic Technique*. New York: Brunner/Mazel, 1983.

McGuire, W. (Ed.). *The Freud and Jung Letters*. Princeton: Bollingen, 1974.

Moore, B., & Fine, B. (Eds.). *Glossary of Psychoanalytic Terms and Concepts*. New York: American Psychoanalytic Association, 1968.

Mullahy, P. *Psychoanalysis and Interpersonal Psychiatry: The Concepts of H. S. Sullivan*. New York: Science House, 1970.

Nowell, E. *Thomas Wolfe, A Biography*. New York: Doubleday, 1960.

Rank, O. *The Trauma of Birth*. New York: Harcourt, Brace, 1929.

Rinsley, D. B. *Treatment of the Severely Disturbed Adolescent*. New York: Jason Aronson, 1980.

Rinsley, D. B. *Borderline and Other Self Disorders: A Developmental-Object Relations Perspective*. New York: Jason Aronson, 1982.

Roth, P. *Portnoy's Complaint*. New York: Random House, 1969.

Sartre, J. *No Exit* (trans. S. Gilbert). New York: Alfred A. Knopf, 1946.

Sartre, J. *The Words*. New York: Fawcett, 1964.

Sartre, J. *Being and Nothingness* (trans. A. Barnes). New York: Simon & Schuster, 1966.

Snow White and the Seven Dwarfs (trans. & illus. W. Gaz). New York: Coward, 1932.

Stang, R. *Edvard Munch*. New York: Abbeville Press, 1977.

Strachey, J. (Ed.), in collaboration with Freud, A. *The Complete Psychological Works of Sigmund Freud*. London: Hogarth Press, 1966.

Turnbull, A. *Thomas Wolfe*. New York: Scribners, 1968.

Winnicott, D. *Ego Distortions in Terms of True and False Self: In the Maturational Processes and the Facilitating Environment*. New York: International Universities Press, 1965.

Wolfe, T. *Look Homeward Angel*. New York: Scribners, 1929.

Wolfe, T. *You Can't Go Home Again*. New York: Harper Bros., 1934.

Wolfe, T. *Of Time and the River*. New York: Scribners, 1935.

Wolfe, T. *The Story of a Novel*. New York: Scribners, 1936.

Wolfe, T. *The Web and the Rock*. New York: Harper Bros., 1937.

Index

179